082130

D0714512

OTHER TITLES IN THIS SERIES:

BY THE SAME AUTHOR:

URSULA MARKHAM

Managing Conflict

Thorsons
An Imprint of HarperCollinsPublishers

Thorsons
An Imprint of HarperCollins*Publishers*
77–85 Fulham Palace Road,
Hammersmith, London W6 8JB
1160 Battery Street,
San Francisco, California 94111-1213

Published by Thorsons 1996
10 9 8 7 6 5 4 3 2 1

A catalogue record for this book
is available from the British Library

ISBN 0 7225 3109 5

Printed in Great Britain by
HarperCollinsManufacturing Glasgow

To my mother and sons

With love

Next to a battle lost, the
greatest misery is a battle gained.

THE DUKE OF WELLINGTON, 1769–1852

Contents

Introduction

Although we tend to think of it as being entirely negative, conflict is not necessarily a bad thing. Provided it does not get out of hand, it can often be useful when trying to solve problems or to find creative ways of improving a situation.

Conflict often arises in those situations where there is considerable freedom of speech and acknowledgement of ideas – and such situations should not be discouraged. Skillful leadership and management, however, can ensure that what exists is *negotiation* rather than actual conflict.

Encouraging negotiation involves many skills, predominant among which is the ability to assess the personality types around you – recognizing the aggressive person who is determined to win now but has little regard for the long-term outcome, the submissive person whose only means of exerting power may be to be uncooperative, and the assertive person who does what he or she can to achieve a win/win outcome.

Although this book deals predominantly with managing conflicts which arise in working life and relationships, the techniques for handling them are very similar when it comes to dealing with your personal life. Hopefully, therefore, when you have put them into practice in as many areas as possible, you will find that you are able to live a happier and more productive life all round.

CHAPTER ONE

Why Conflict Arises

In any environment where you find a number of people having to work together and relate to one another, there is bound to be conflict. This would be the case even in the event that each and every member of a group had nothing but their company's best interests at heart.

The type of discussion and exchange of views which takes place because people have differing opinions about what should be done or how to approach a specific task can be extremely useful to a company. Indeed, many innovative and successful ideas have come about as a result of this type of informal brainstorming. In addition they do not cause feelings of personal malice, as no one is criticizing or disagreeing with an individual as a person but with his or her ideas – therefore no offence should be taken.

What frequently happens, however, is that such exchanges *do* become highly personal and the effects of negative remarks directed to one or more of the people concerned last long after the particular problem has been solved and forgotten.

Imagine yourself in such a situation. Suppose you put forward what you consider to be a good idea which is likely to be of benefit to the company or to solve a particular problem which has arisen. How would you respond to each of the following?:

'*I don't really think that idea would work because...*'
'*Don't be so stupid; that can't possibly work.*'

The second comment would leave you feeling foolish and

inferior – and probably determined never to put forward a suggestion again. The first, however, seems to be telling you that your idea was worth considering but that, after consideration, it does not seem to be appropriate. The fact that someone then goes on to explain to you just why this is so helps you to feel that you are a person entitled to such explanation and therefore part of the team as a whole. As a result of what is said you may be able to modify your original idea and come up with a better one but, even if not, you will not feel diffident or disheartened about putting forward another suggestion in the future.

If you think about it, it is natural – and almost inevitable – for conflict to arise in any place where a group of individuals from diverse backgrounds and with different expectations and experiences are put together. A few years ago, realizing this, some organizations attempted to staff their offices and places of work with people of similar types and backgrounds – often sorting them out by means of psychometric or similar testing at the interview stage. However, it was found that this often resulted in the type of workplace where no one appeared to demonstrate great enthusiasm for the job or to put forward innovative or positive suggestions.

It is now appreciated by most companies that there is great benefit in having staff from differing backgrounds and with different personalities – provided the supervisor or team leader understands how to manage them to get the best out of them while providing an atmosphere with as little personal friction as possible.

Differences in background are more than those of culture, race, education, etc. – which are relatively easy to assess. It is possible to have two people with very similar cultural backgrounds who, because they have been affected in different ways by their life experiences, respond in diversely different ways to the same situation.

Jonathan and Martin both worked in the office of a design company. Although neither of them was actually employed as a designer, the company was a small one and it was expected that everyone would put forward ideas and contribute to the company's growth and success.

On the surface both young men came from similar backgrounds. Each had been brought up in the suburbs of London within families who, although not extremely wealthy, had a comfortable lifestyle and wanted for little. Each boy had attended a local preparatory school and then the local grammar school before going on to university. We would be forgiven, therefore, for assuming that their reactions to specific situations were likely to be very similar – although this was far from the case.

Jonathan came from a family which allowed everyone to develop his or her own personality and, apart from normal everyday family frictions, he had been quite happy as a child. He had always been encouraged to express his views, provided he did so reasonably and provided he was also willing to listen to the views of the others. If a problem arose or there was a difference of views, a family conference would be held where the opinions of Jonathan, his parents and his brothers and sister were all listened to, discussed and considered before a communal decision was reached.

In this way Jonathan became aware from a very early age that it was quite possible to disagree with those you loved and respected, and that this disagreement would not be detrimental to those feelings. He also realized, over a period of time, that he did not always get his way but that, provided his ideas were reasonable, every now and again he would do so. He also grew to appreciate that sometimes other people's ideas – even those with which he originally disagreed – could turn out to be for the best.

Martin's parents had a very different view of the best way to bring up their son. The only child of older parents, he had always been aware that a great deal was expected of him. It was taken for granted that he would do well at school – and, indeed, by a combination of hard work and aptitude, he did. But the effort was never appreciated; the boy was never praised. However, if he did slightly less well in any examination or if the comment on his report was not as favourable as his parents would have liked, he was shouted at, criticized, belittled and told that he was letting down the family.

Because he was an only child and because his parents were not particularly sociable, Martin did not find it easy to make friends either at school or later. With people of his own age he appeared shy and awkward, while with anyone in a position of authority he was either over-anxious to please or he managed to persuade them that the task they set was beyond his capabilities and so he made himself out to be far less able than he really was.

Once they were in the office situation, the differences in attitude between Jonathan and Martin became very noticeable. Jonathan was easy-going and willing to listen to other people's views but also determined to make his own known. Martin, on the other hand, had such a low opinion of himself and his ideas that he never proposed any suggestions at all in case they were ridiculed or shouted down. This was a great pity as he was a bright young man and actually had some innovative and workable ideas which never saw the light of day.

This failure to contribute only served to increase Martin's sense of inferiority and to reduce his self-esteem even further. To make himself feel better he began criticizing any proposals put forward by others in the office and ridiculing those who had made them. He believed that this made him sound interested and knowledgeable, whereas to everyone else he appeared negative and obstructive and they soon learned to keep well away from him. Thus his sense of isolation increased and a vicious circle was formed.

Personality Types

You will find, in any group of people working together, that each individual has different needs. One person may see the job as a necessary evil – something to do during the day in order to take home a weekly or monthly pay cheque. Another may be fascinated by the work itself and be determined to do the very best he can while there – even if he is able to put it out of his mind during holidays and weekends. A third person may be highly ambitious and anxious to seize every opportunity to show what she can do, possibly seeing the current job as a stepping-stone to greater and higher things.

The last of these is known as a Type-A personality. Two cardiologists, Dr Ray Rosenman and Dr Meyer Friedman, divided people into Type-A and Type-B personalities. The work of these doctors was concerned with susceptibility to heart disease but, if you look at the characteristics of each type, you will see that they are also going to react very differently to possible conflict situations.

CHARACTERISTICS OF A TYPE-A PERSONALITY

- actively seeks promotion at work or advancement socially
- is highly competitive
- has a strong, often domineering personality
- desires public recognition for his or her efforts
- loses his or her temper easily
- becomes restless when compelled to be inactive
- does everything quickly – speaking, walking, moving, eating, etc.
- loves to have several jobs on the go at once
- is very conscious of time – thrives on deadlines
- grows impatient with others who are not as quick as him- or herself
- is always punctual.

CHARACTERISTICS OF A TYPE-B PERSONALITY

- tackles tasks slowly and methodically
- is rarely competitive – whether working or playing
- likes to do a job well but does not desire public recognition
- speaks quite slowly and has an easy-going manner
- is not particularly ambitious
- does not lose his or her temper easily
- prefers to tackle one task at a time
- enjoys periods of idleness
- moves unhurriedly
- is not time-conscious – may miss deadlines or arrive late.

Very few people fit exactly into one category, but most are predominantly Type A or Type B. And, if you look at the characteristics listed you will see how, without effective management, it would be quite easy for conflict to arise when both were employed in the same workplace.

Although, on the surface, the Type-A person appears to be the more difficult to deal with, none the less these are people we really need. They are the ones who will stick with a job and ensure that it gets done; they are the ones who are most likely to have the innovative ideas; they are the ones who will 'bully' everyone else into meeting that important deadline. And, in many cases, they are the ones who go far in their chosen field.

If Type-A personalities can be given the right amount of responsibility but urged to temper their natural impatience when others may not act or react as quickly as they do, they can make excellent team leaders. However, if this 'tempering' does not take place, they can soon cause friction within a group.

Because you will be dealing with different types of people, if conflict is to be avoided it is essential to be able to recognize these types from the outset and deal with each individually, realizing that each has its good and bad points.

Aggressive, Submissive and Assertive Personalities

Type A personalities are always aggressive; Type B people are usually either assertive or submissive. Each of these three categories will be clearly recognizable from a person's speech and attitudes. But even before this – often within the first few minutes of meeting someone – his (or her) body language should make it clear to you into which category he falls. You can then form an opinion about how he will fit in with an existing group, the best way in which to handle him in order to bring out his positive attributes – and even whether he is the type of person you actually want.

How to Recognize an Aggressive Person

BODY LANGUAGE
- very stiff and straight
- stares fixedly
- inclined to point, jab a finger, bang the table, etc. to emphasize a point
- folds arms across body

VERBAL LANGUAGE
because the aggressive person is convinced that he (or she) is the one in the right, his language tends to bear this out. He will say such things as:

- 'I want you to...'
- 'You must...'
- 'Do what I tell you!'
- 'You're stupid!'

As you will gather from the above, the aggressive person is not popular. Aggression of this sort is akin to bullying, and while bullies may be feared – and even obeyed – they are never liked or respected. The aggressive person may get his own way in the short term, but he will never command long-term loyalty from those around him. He (and of course this can apply to either sex) often traps himself in a vicious circle of his own making. He tends to be somewhat of a loner who does not really like himself or other people. Having a constant need to reassure his inner self that he is the wonderful person he would dearly like to be, he usually becomes highly critical of those around him, desperately trying to convince them – and himself at the same time – that he is as near perfect as it is possible to be. Because this naturally alienates others, they keep out of his way as much as possible, increasing his sense of isolation and loneliness and making him act in an even more aggressive manner.

One thing to bear in mind is that – just as the physical bully is really a coward – the aggressive person is basically insecure.

No one with even a reasonable amount of confidence feels the need to be aggressive towards others.

If you wish to avoid conflict around you, it is best to have as little to do with truly aggressive people as possible. If you have no choice in the matter and find that you must interact with someone highly aggressive, you will need to be ever watchful and to do what you can to minimize the repercussions of his behaviour.

How to Recognize a Submissive Person

BODY LANGUAGE
- avoids eye contact
- has a stooping posture
- speaks either very quietly or in a whining tone
- backs away when spoken to
- fidgets – wringing hands or plucking at clothes

VERBAL LANGUAGE
Because the submissive person has such a sense of inferiority that he (or she) believes everyone else is right and he is always wrong, he is forever apologizing. Typical expressions include:

- 'I'm sorry to bother you but…'
- 'Oh dear'
- 'It's all my fault'

The submissive person also has a great sense of inferiority, believing he has nothing whatsoever to offer. And, should he work in close contact with an aggressive person, he will be easily destroyed by the latter's criticism and obvious contempt. It can be quite exhausting trying to work with a submissive person and to convince him of his worth. However, it may well be worth persevering as, once his confidence grows, he can be a loyal and trustworthy worker.

Unfortunately – before you reach that stage – the extremely submissive person may cause friction among those around him.

Although in theory everyone wants to help the underdog, none the less it can be very irritating indeed to deal with someone whose negativity is so overwhelming that it seems impossible to penetrate.

How to Recognize an Assertive Person

BODY LANGUAGE
- stands straight but in a relaxed way
- appears composed
- maintains eye contact without staring fixedly
- smiles

VERBAL LANGUAGE
The assertive person will have respect for himself and for those around him – whether or not he agrees with their opinions. His ideal is to achieve a solution in which everyone wins and, to that end, he is prepared to compromise or negotiate if necessary. His language demonstrates this:

- 'Let's...'
- 'How shall we do this?'
- 'I think...what do you think?'
- 'I would like...'

The assertive person really does want the best for himself and for the other person too. He does not seek all the glory for himself, nor does he stab others in the back. In an ideal world, you would do what you could to surround yourself with assertive people. If this were possible, conflicts would never arise; there would be discussions and exchanges of views followed by negotiation and (if necessary) some compromise until everyone was happy with the outcome.

But this is not an ideal world and you are not going to find yourself surrounded by assertive people. But with some careful and caring management from you, those around you can be helped to become more assertive and less negative, as the various chapters in this book will demonstrate.

Perhaps the best way to start is to take time to consider the actual personality types of those around you now. It takes very little time to complete a basic assessment form (as illustrated below) for each person. But, having done so and having taken into consideration the other people with whom each person works, you may be able to see where and why conflict is likely to arise.

When assessing someone's personality, do be careful not to take a single isolated sign as having too great a meaning. Someone may have his arms folded because he is cold; his voice could be quiet because he has a sore throat. Use your judgement and take into account as many different signs as possible.

Name:

Position:

Type A/Type B:

Aggressive/submissive/assertive:

Works in close contact with:

Another of the causes of conflict in any work environment is the rigid adherence to a plan which has been decided upon – sometimes by those who are not personally involved in the particular task – without taking into account the personalities concerned. No plan is carved in stone; there is always the possibility of adaptation in order to make it more suitable for the personnel who will be doing the work.

I am not trying to pretend that such adaptation will not involve a plethora of management skills. As the person who has to resolve the situation, you will be called on to act as mediator, motivator and team-builder, but none of these roles is beyond your capabilities and the results you will achieve will more than make up for any extra time and effort on your part. In the chapters to come you will discover how to use these skills to ensure that conflict is kept to a minimum and that tasks are completed as quickly and efficiently as possible while the workforce remains positive and enthusiastic.

CHAPTER TWO

The Different Types of Conflict

It is possible for some forms of conflict to be responsible for bringing about positive results by:

POSITIVES OF CONFLICT

- encouraging those involved to talk *to* one another rather than to gossip *about* one another;
- possibly being the means of ousting out-dated habits and techniques in favour of newer and more satisfactory ones;
- making the workplace more pleasant by promoting compromise so that everyone is able to gain some satisfaction from the outcome. This can only occur, of course, if the conflict is properly managed in the first place.

Remember that, even when the problem appears to be about concepts, methods, techniques or ideologies, all conflict is about people and the relationships between them.

There are obviously many types of conflict, but they can all manifest themselves on one of four different levels:

1) within an individual
2) between two individuals
3) within a team of individuals
4) between two or more teams within an organization.

We will now look at each of these levels in more detail.

Within One Individual

POSITIVE?

This can have a positive or negative outcome. If the conflict goes on in someone's head and concerns different methods of achieving a proposed outcome – and analysing and selecting the best method – then it can be a source of invention and creativity.

Many celebrated thinkers and inventors have taken their time when reaching a desired solution – often appearing to become morose and introspective in the mean time. If you know someone, on however great or small a scale, who is this type of thinker and who likes to mull over a problem before voicing her (or his) solution to it, the only thing to do is leave her alone to get on with it. If you interrupt her train of thought she might either accept a lesser solution to the problem or even give up working on it altogether.

In a negative sense, the individual might well be worrying whether some action which is expected of her is not the right thing to do or whether she is being asked to do something which is in direct opposition to her principles.

Eleanor worked for a thriving advertising agency in London. She was still quite young but had built up a sound reputation, being acknowledged as extremely innovative and creative. Because of this reputation, on many occasions a client of her company would request that she be put in personal charge of its account.

One day the agency was approached by one of the country's leading cosmetic companies, who were about to launch a new range of products and were anxious for Eleanor to plan their whole campaign.

The problem arose because this particular company made no secret of the fact that their products were tested on animals, and this was something to which Eleanor personally objected. Thus a serious conflict was aroused in her mind:

On the one hand, she was being approached as an experienced professional to do a job at which she was expert.

On the other hand, she was not sure that she would be able to put heart and soul into a campaign which was so against her personal beliefs – or even whether she should even begin to try.

As she struggled to make up her mind, various points came to her:

- The offer was extremely tempting, not only because of the money she personally would be able to command, but because her prestige and reputation would be considerably enhanced if she made a good job of it.
- She owed a considerable amount of loyalty to the agency, which had taken her on when she was young and unknown and had nurtured and trained her until she had attained her present level of expertise. If she turned down the commission, it was quite possible that the cosmetics company would take their business (including any which might arise in the future) elsewhere.
- She found the whole idea of testing cosmetics on animals so abhorrent that she did not know whether she would even be capable of working on the campaign. She had always gone out of her way to avoid similar commissions in the past.
- Working on the possibility that she would take on the job and do it really well, she personally might be responsible for a greatly increased sale of the cosmetics and this in turn might lead to even more products requiring even more animal suffering.

Eleanor was in torment. As time passed and the day approached when she had to give her answer, she became more and more confused. There simply was no satisfactory conclusion to this particular conflict. Not only that, but she spent so much time thinking about it that her current work began to suffer.

While both forms of internal conflict can cause an individual to become temporarily introverted or self-possessed as she seeks a solution, the difference lies in the outcome. While, in the case of the first scenario – searching for a new way to achieve some goal – will eventually prove, in many cases, to have been worth the anguish, the second situation – the one in which Eleanor found herself – is not really capable of being satisfactorily resolved. Whatever solution she comes to, there will always be an element of dissatisfaction – of having let herself, her ideals or other people down. There is no easy answer; all anyone can do is make the best decision he or she can in the circumstances.

Between Two Individuals

Whether this sort of conflict arises within a work situation or in someone's personal life, it is always destructive to a relationship. Not only does it cause often permanent resentment between the two people concerned, it also makes life extremely difficult for anyone who has to work with or come into close contact with either or both of them. At best, it creates an uncomfortable daily situation; at worst, others find themselves taking sides with one or other of the people concerned, and so friction can build up between two opposing 'factions'. For these reasons it needs to be dealt with as swiftly as possible.

Felix was always late. He would arrive in the office five minutes after everyone else – although seemingly oblivious of the fact. His coffee and lunch breaks regularly seemed to take a few minutes longer than other people's. He began to pack up in the evening sufficiently early to ensure that he was out of the office on the dot of 5.30. While he was there and actually working, he worked as hard and appeared to achieve as much as anyone else. But the fact remained that – even if it was only a few minutes here and there – he did cut corners with his timekeeping.

This didn't seem to bother anyone too much. Felix was a likable person and he usually managed to do what was asked of him. Then, one day, he was asked to work on a joint project with Sally.

Sally was a prompt and efficient worker who was always at her desk on time. The first morning of the new project Felix arrived at the office to find Sally already at her desk. She was tapping her fingers impatiently on the table but she said nothing as Felix got ready for the day. The same situation arose after lunch and after the tea and coffee breaks. At 5.20, just after they had begun to work on a new phase of the project, Felix leapt to his feet and insisted that he had to go.

Still Sally managed not to say anything. But when the same thing happened the next and every subsequent day, she began to grow really annoyed. Eventually she could stand it no longer and launched a verbal attack on Felix, complaining that she was expected to do a lot more work for the same money and the same amount of recognition that he was getting.

Felix couldn't understand what the problem was. He managed to achieve everything he set out to do every day. But the more he tried to reason with Sally, the more irritated she became. Eventually the atmosphere between them was so unfriendly – made worse by the fact that they were compelled to work together – that it affected everyone else in the office. Disagreements broke out as, one after another, people took sides with either Felix or Sally. Soon these disagreements spread to incorporate every kind of situation within the office.

———————

Within a Team of Individuals

If you have a team of people working in a creative (as opposed to mechanical) way, then natural conflict of ideas is bound to arise all the time. When this is channelled into positive brainstorming sessions, then innovative new ideas and concepts may be put forward. But such sessions should be run in a controlled and organized fashion and for a specified amount of time only.

This works well provided only ideas are involved. Once personalities find their way into the arena, the situation becomes far more difficult to control. If it causes disruption in the team, then that team's performance is bound to suffer.

When several people are involved in a department or in a particular project, it is essential that they are encouraged to sit round a table and discuss ideas and doubts – whether or not a proper brainstorming session is held. It is when isolated conversations between groups of two or three people are held that confusion and misunderstanding arise and conflict may be caused.

Another disadvantage of such small pockets of discussion is that one individual may take part in several of them and, depending upon his (or her) personality, may appear to be either in favour of all or against all.

Andrew was the most junior member of his team. He had only been with the organization for a short time and, although his work was good and he showed considerable promise for the future, his level of confidence was not great. He was conscious that some of the other members of the team were both dynamic and innovative and this, coupled with their years of experience, caused Andrew to feel unsure of himself. He enjoyed the job; he liked the other people and he desperately wanted to acquit himself well.

Whenever Andrew came upon a group of two or three members of the team discussing a particular project and was asked for his opinion, he would agree with the suggestions they were putting forward – not really having the courage to do otherwise. He didn't think this would cause any problems until he heard someone with whom he'd had a discussion the previous day saying to another team member, 'Well, Tom, Sheila and Andrew agree with me.' In fact he had not really agreed – he had simply avoided giving an opinion or taking part in the discussion at all. But suddenly he found himself in one of two opposing camps – something which had never been his intention.

In this particular instance the matter was of little importance and so the conflict remained minimal. But, had the same situation occurred when the subject under discussion was far more critical, Andrew could have found himself apparently supporting something he was not in favour of, and even possibly antagonizing some of his colleagues simply because he had wanted to please everyone.

Between Two Teams in the Same Organization

Some companies actively encourage conflict and competition between teams of workers within their organization, believing that this will result in each team performing more effectively and achieving greater results while seeking to outdo the other. Sometimes this may be so but, unless the situation is carefully monitored, there is always the danger that the sense of competition will become more important than the final outcome of the work being undertaken. If this should happen, the scenario should be changed immediately and efforts made to channel everyone's energies – particularly those who are most competitive – in a different way.

Taken to extremes and depending upon the personalities of the people involved, competition between teams can lead to members of one group deliberately sabotaging the efforts of the other, so great is their desire to win. While this may at first seem amusing to the rivals, it doesn't take long for the situation to get out of hand and for good-humoured mischief-making to turn into malicious destruction. None of this is of any benefit at all to an organization. At the very least it is a waste of time and effort; taken to extremes it can cause the complete disintegration of the workforce.

Causes of Conflict

All the classes of conflict mentioned are probably going on all the time in any organization – but usually in such a minor way that the effects are so slight as to be unnoticeable.

Bearing in mind these four levels at which conflict most commonly occurs, let's have a look at some of the most common reasons for it.

Conflict of Aims

This is most likely to arise when one or more people has a different goal in mind. This situation may have arisen because of a simple misunderstanding – perhaps they were not all told at the same time what was required, and a slight variation in phrase has caused them to have a different interpretation of the instructions given. Or perhaps the explanation itself was not as clear as it might have been and either the person giving it did not allow time for questions and other forms of feedback or those who were listening felt too self-conscious or nervous to query what had been said.

If something new is being introduced, you may come up against those who naturally resent change of any sort. This is actually quite common – in all aspects of life – so it is important that the changes are suggested in such a way that the listener believes them to be to her (or his) advantage to take them on board. Dale Carnegie used to incorporate into his teachings the concept that, in order to sell – whether an item, an idea or oneself – you should always 'talk in terms of the other person's interest.' In other words, not 'these widgets are the best ever invented' but 'by using these widgets you will gain so much free time.'

Resentment of change is very common in all areas of life because it takes considerable effort. Most people prefer to stick with what they know – even when they realize that what they know is not particularly good for them. But, with perseverance, once the benefits of a change are appreciated it doesn't actually take very long for habits and attitudes to adapt themselves to the change.

If you want to prove this to yourself in a light-hearted way, try shifting the position of your wastepaper basket. If it is always to the right of your desk, put it to the left. You will probably spend the first few days throwing all your rubbish on the floor on the right-hand side of your desk, but within a week or two you will be happily tossing it in the bin on your left without even thinking about it.

Another manifestation of a conflict of aims is when different individuals have open differences about the desired goal. One may be determined to preserve the status quo at all costs while another is always seeking better and different ways of doing things. Or perhaps one is really only interested in doing her job as well as possible but not in anything else. Sometimes an underlying resentment can cause subtle behaviour changes designed to resist change at all costs.

Such negativity in a single individual is like a stone being thrown into a pool of water. It doesn't take long before the ripples spread through the team, completely sabotaging the desired outcome planned by the organization.

Conflict of Ideas

Because of many aspects of their backgrounds, different people will place a different interpretation on the same words. This is why feedback in the form of paraphrasing or questioning is so essential (this will be covered in detail in Chapter 5). To give an example, I recently attended a meeting where an American employer was talking about one of his staff and said that 'if he doesn't buck his ideas up, I'm going to terminate him.' He couldn't understand why the British people there found this so amusing. After all, he only meant that he was going to fire him. And had he said 'terminate his employment' or 'terminate his contract' that would have been perfectly clear. But – particularly after films such as *Terminator* – many people construe the word 'terminate' as 'murder'.

Now of course we all knew that this man didn't intend to kill his unsatisfactory employee; we understood what he meant but it was still amusing – and still had to be explained to him!

Suppose, however, instead of this fairly casual expression the American gentleman had been explaining how he wanted a particular task completed and had used a phrase which was perfectly clear to him but which was capable of being misinterpreted by one or more of those listening to him. And suppose he had not demanded any feedback from those to whom he was speaking – what then? Plans could have been drawn up, systems initiated and tasks undertaken, all of which were based on an entirely false premise.

Such situations are caused by differences not only in language but in a listener's previous experience, educational background, nervousness and the speed at which she can take in new information. But these situations can at least be foreseen and therefore the conflict which could arise from them is avoidable.

Conflict of ideas can also arise when a new member joins an existing team. However skilled this person may be, her (or his) ideas are bound to differ in some way from those of a group used to working together. Depending entirely upon how such a situation is handled, it can be extremely beneficial as it can inject a dose of new thinking into a group which may have become a little stale. On the other hand, it can have devastating results if the existing team-members resent the way the newcomer voices her ideas, and decide to set about opposing them as a matter of principle rather than because the ideas lack merit.

If it is suggested – whether to an individual or to a team – that a new method of working should be introduced, conflict may arise. Whatever the suggestions, there will always be someone who believes – rightly or wrongly – that the old ways are the best.

Conflict of Attitude

This is by far the most difficult type of conflict to resolve, as it often concerns the deep-rooted feelings and opinions of one or more individuals within a group. These feelings and opinions might have a political, cultural, racial or gender-biased background and may have been part of the make-up of that person for many years. People holding such beliefs are not only convinced that they are right – they simply cannot understand why everyone else does not see things the way they do. They certainly have no intention of changing and would demonstrate

21

strong resistance to anyone who tried to force them to do so.

In such situations there is little anyone can do apart from finding a means of separating those who are in such conflict.

Conflict of Behaviour

This arises when one or more of the people involved behaves in a way which others find unacceptable. Perhaps this is someone who is *never* on time for an appointment, who refuses to co-operate when new ideas are suggested or who doesn't pull her weight within a team. It is most commonly a single individual who is the focus of the resentment, although sometimes the same situation can arise when one team among a group of teams becomes difficult or obstructive.

The Four Stages of Conflict

Whatever its initial cause, conflict seems to pass through a particular cycle consisting of four main stages.

Let's look at these four stages by following the course of a common conflict: It is time for the annual pay review in a medium-sized manufacturing company which has been doing quite well over recent years. The workforce believe that a particular pay rise would be appropriate, while management is determined to give far less.

Stage One

The members of the workforce are angry and frustrated when their request is turned down – particularly as they genuinely believe that they deserve it and that management should recognize this. Their anger may lead to the choosing of a leader, and that person may well organize a confrontation between the parties.

Stage Two

Each side has to work out several points if they are to present their respective cases coherently and forcefully.

1. What Is the Problem?
In this example, the workforce feels that it is not being adequately recompensed for the amount of effort put in.

Management, for their part, has decided upon what it thinks is a fair rate of increase, bearing in mind future plans and viability of the company.

2. What Outcome Would They Like to See?
The workforce want the management to increase the amount offered, thereby proving that management appreciates the efforts that have been made on the company's behalf.

Management want to give a smaller increase. This may be for many reasons. Perhaps the company is in financial difficulty and may be forced to cut back or introduce redundancies if extremely high wage rises are met; or perhaps the directors simply feel that they want to give away as little as possible.

3. How Are They Prepared to Compromise if Necessary?
The workforce may have put in a claim for a larger wage increase than they expect to receive, realizing that management will do all they can to knock them down. They may now be prepared to reduce their claim slightly – although not to what is on the table.

Experience having taught them that the above is likely to be the case, management may now be prepared to offer slightly more than previously – although not what the workers are claiming as their due.

4. How Are They Going to Set about Achieving Their Aims?
Here there may be many variations depending upon the temperament and the strength of feeling among members of the workforce – and also upon whether or not there have been similar

conflicts in the past and how they were resolved. They might decide upon anything from across-the-table talks with management to withdrawal of overtime or even out-and-out strike action.

The decision of the management team might also be to take one of several different actions. They too might prefer verbal negotiation or – if they are really determined not to give an inch – they may choose to sit back and see how far the members of the workforce are prepared to go.

5. How Are Current Strategy and Decisions Likely to Affect any Possible Future Conflicts which May Arise over the Same Subject?
Here both sides may feel that, if they are seen to give in too easily, they are setting an unfortunate precedent for the future. They are likely to want to be seen to be determined but not deliberately obstructive to the point where either the benefit to the workforce or to the organization itself is damaged. We have all heard of cases where strikes have been so bitter and protracted that, even when some extra concessions have been gained, it is unlikely that the individuals concerned were ever going to recoup their losses. In the same way, no company can afford to hold out for so long that they lose business which it may be extremely difficult to regain.

Stage Three

This involves each side putting their chosen plan – or part one of it – into action. The result may be talks, refusal to work overtime, threats of strike action on the one hand and dismissal on the other or even the occurrence of actual strikes or dismissals.

Stage Four

This stage is reached when an actual result has been achieved – and this will usually be some form of compromise between the two parties. A great deal now depends upon attitudes and the amount of goodwill that remains. Either each side will have to accept the compromise – with all that it tells them about their future – or one side will be left feeling dissatisfied and therefore far more prone to further conflict, whether over a similar or completely different problem.

If the workforce, in this particular example, decides to be pleased with what they have achieved in the way of an increase over the offer originally made, they will work more effectively and have more loyalty to the company than if they consider the situation as a loss on their part. If they are not pleased with the outcome, this can only lead to resentment – and therefore more conflict – in the future.

Management can either decide to find ways in which they can accept any compromise which may have been reached or they can allow their resentment of the fact that they have been compelled to find more money than they would have wished to make them see the workforce as the 'enemy', to be thwarted whenever possible.

The example given here is a basic one which arises time and time again in companies large and small – but the stages indicated are the same whatever the cause of the conflict which arises.

If you are the person in charge when a conflict does arise – whether between individuals or groups – it is up to you to watch for the commencement of this cycle and to try and do something about it during Stage 2. Once this point has been passed, things becomes far more difficult. Tempers may well be raised and obstinacy may set in where one or more of the parties concerned refuses to consider the idea of compromise in any way.

Both sides are likely to become less reasonable over time, and it is almost impossible to get an aggressively angry person to resolve conflict amicably.

If negative conflict is not caught and dispersed in time, long-term problems may arise. Individuals vary in the way they react to bitter conflict. Many become so stressed that, even when the conflict itself has been resolved, their work and attitude continue to suffer. This, of course, gives everyone an additional problem to deal with.

How Different
Personality Types Handle Conflict

Naturally there are some people who are confident enough to understand the importance of negotiation and compromise from the outset – but such people are usually in the minority. Many are either aggressive or submissive – either of which can create problems for the whole team.

THE AGGRESSIVE PERSON

- This person may set herself up as a ringleader, attempting to persuade colleagues to join a go-slow or a strike or to practise some other method of deliberate uncooperativeness. She (or he) will spend a great deal of time talking to others – often less dogmatic than herself – in an attempt to persuade them to come round to her way of thinking.

- An aggressive person is also stubborn and will refuse to change her mind. She feels that having to 'lose face' or 'climb down' (as she sees it) would make her less of a person in the eyes of her colleagues.

- She may become generally aggressive in all matters. If she feels she is not able to get her own way or to vent her anger on those with whom she has been in conflict, she will often turn on those people least able to cope with her aggressive attitude. This is a form of bullying which can create great problems in any team as other members attempt either to join ranks with the aggressor or to restrain her.

THE SUBMISSIVE PERSON

- The submissive person may become apathetic, obeying orders and carrying out her (or his) job but not really thinking about what she is doing. It may appear on the surface that this sort of individual is far less trouble than someone who is aggressive – but in the long term she is really of minimal value to any organization while she continues to act in this way.

- The tension and stress experienced by a submissive person when forced to become involved in a conflict situation can cause her to become physically ill. Although the cause of the illness may be emotional, none the less the condition is perfectly genuine. Some of the most common problems which arise in such circumstances include insomnia, migraine, backache, ulcers, high blood-pressure, hyper-anxiety as well as stress-induced aches and pains. Unless something can be done about the underlying emotional causes for such conditions, they are likely not only to persist but to become worse, possibly culminating in the long-term absenteeism of the person concerned.

- As a result of being involved in conflict the submissive person may become increasingly absent-minded. You can see how damaging this could be to her work – and therefore to the organization – as she repeatedly forgets what she has been told, where she has put things or what she is supposed to do next. Such an individual may also develop a tendency to daydream while at work – which is her way of cutting out possible sources of friction rather in the same way that many depressives sleep for a greater part of the day in order to shut out the problems of their world.

- An extremely able submissive person may seek refuge in pretending to be far less skilled or knowledgeable than she is. By doing this, she effectively withdraws herself from the 'battle zone' and avoids – so she hopes – being asked to do anything remotely concerned with the area of conflict.

- In extreme cases when there is frequent conflict with which she feels unable to cope, the submissive person will simply leave the company altogether.

Conflict Caused by Hostile Personalities

Some people have a permanently hostile attitude towards the world in general and, even though this may have nothing at all to do with their work, these people themselves can be responsible for creating areas of conflict where none might otherwise exist.

There could be many reasons for this hostile attitude. Perhaps the sufferer is going through a particularly difficult time at home, with relationship problems or having to cope with difficult children. Some may be trying to cope with great financial worries – often while attempting to hide this fact from others.

If they have problems but feel helpless in the face of them and unable to cope, such people may well come to work in a bad temper, ready to be obstructive at the first opportunity.

Of course some anxieties exist because of work itself. Fear of redundancy is rampant today and an individual may be too scared of losing status – or even employment – to speak freely to those in management. This brings about a sense of frustration and, there being no one else to take it out on, colleagues are made to suffer. As you will realize, this is hardly conducive to a happy working team.

Sometimes it just happens that one member of a team dislikes another – perhaps for no apparent reason but because of a clash of two distinct personalities. It is not always possible to do anything to rectify such a situation so, particularly if each person is valued for the particular skills he or she brings to work, dealing with the conflicts that will inevitably arise between them is time-consuming and not always easy.

Some 'instant dislikes' are, of course, the result of prejudice on the part of one of the individuals concerned. Here great care must be taken when dealing the problem, as any form of prejudice against another person because of race, creed or colour is unlawful and must be dealt with quickly and effectively.

Depending upon the particular circumstances involved, in the case of personal prejudice – for whatever reason – it is often advisable to see if there is any way of ensuring that the people concerned are not compelled to work in close proximity for longer than absolutely necessary. No one is ever going to change the mind of a bigot – and it is very difficult to sack someone on a charge of bigotry. The manager, whatever his or her own views, must keep the workplace as harmonious as possible, so keeping the parties separate is probably the best he or she can do.

There may be times when you will encounter hostility between various members of a single team. If this is a group of people each bringing his or her skills to working on a particular project, it will obviously be impractical to try separating them all. Ob-viously it is necessary to talk to them about the situation, but it is essential to talk to them all at once if you are not to make it worse. When people are already feeling negative, they may see it as a slight if they are not the first to be approached. In addition, however much you might think you are saying the same thing to everyone, in such situations any difference in words or tones may be seized upon and its meaning exaggerated.

There will also be times when you become aware that a conflict situation has arisen but you have no idea as to the cause. This is the time to exercise all your managerial skills and become the best communicator you can be. Be there, be approachable – and let everyone realize that you are. Make them understand that they can talk to you, singly or together, formally or on an informal basis.

Do your best not to pre-judge any issue and never to be seen to take sides. (This can be very difficult when you like one individual better than another or when one set of ideas accords more readily with your own.) The importance of not only being impartial but being *seen* to be impartial will stand you in good stead should future conflicts arise.

Misunderstandings

Misunderstandings are quite a common source of conflict, particularly in larger companies where explanations are made and orders issued to groups of people at a time. If it is at all feasible, try to explain things to everyone at once – giving ample opportunity for feedback and questions and remembering that different people have different rates of absorbing new information. Let all the communication skills to be detailed in Chapter 5 come to the fore.

Even when you do all this, allow for the fact that some people are naturally quicker or more intelligent than others.

Some start with a basic pre-knowledge while others may come to a particular task with no real background at all. Just because someone is slower to take in new facts does not mean that she (or he) will not be able to do her work just as well as anyone else – if not better – when she fully understands what is expected of her.

You have seen that conflict can arise for a myriad of different reasons but, once you have learned to recognize the early warning signs, you should be able to use your skills to prevent it escalating into a harmful or distressing situation.

CHAPTER THREE

Internal Conflict

All thinking people suffer from internal conflicts from time to time – but it is only those who have poor levels of confidence or particularly low self-esteem who are not able to resolve them. Whatever the problem and whatever the decision to be made, if you are sure of yourself and what you consider to be right, you should have little difficulty in coming to the right conclusion.

This chapter deals with *you* – the development of your personal self-esteem. It should also help you to appreciate your own value as a worthwhile human being and the special place you hold in the world. If this sounds a mammoth task – or if your opinion of yourself is a little shaky right now, at the end of the chapter you will find various techniques which will help to convince you of your worth and boost your self-esteem.

If you are to be able to manage other people – particularly at difficult times – it is essential to be able to understand and manage your own personal difficulties. This is impossible if you are consumed by doubt as to your own abilities or have little belief in your own value. Nor can you manage successfully if you are full of fear, as fear left unquenched will always increase in intensity. You will eventually reach the stage where you spend your time waiting for your inadequacies (whether real or imagined) to be discovered by other people.

Before you can make changes in yourself, however, it is essential to understand your present position. Look at the statements below and mark any that usually apply to you – remembering that anyone can have an isolated negative day and concentrating on what is normal for you. (As with many questionnaires of this sort, you can make an educated guess as to the most desirable answers. But try to answer as honestly as possible – there is no other way in which to help yourself.)

PERSONAL LIFE

I usually maintain a positive outlook on life. ☐
I enjoy the company of other people. ☐
I find it easy to form relationships. ☐
I wake up feeling good about the coming day. ☐
I am not afraid to show my emotions. ☐
I am able to say no when appropriate. ☐
I can be content when on my own. ☐
I am able to put my mistakes behind me. ☐
I enjoy trying something new. ☐
I like myself. ☐

WORK LIFE

I get on well with my superiors at work. ☐
I get on well with those under me. ☐
I get on well with my colleagues. ☐
I enjoy taking responsibility. ☐
I communicate effectively with others. ☐
I feel confident when issuing instructions or
   giving explanations. ☐
I believe I have the respect of those around me. ☐
I am good at my job. ☐
I am able to put any past mistakes behind me. ☐
I consider myself of value to the company. ☐

Now, unless you are a saint it is unlikely that you were able to agree with each and every one of those statements. But you should, on any given day, be able to say that seven out of the ten in each section apply to you. If you can't, then you need to do some work on yourself in order do so.

Having thought about those statements, please go on to

answer the following:

What do I consider to be my best qualities...
...in my personal life?

1. ....
....
2. ....
....
3. ....
....

...in my working life?

1. ....
....
2. ....
....
3. ....
....

What do I consider to be my worst qualities...
...in my personal life?

1. ....
....
2. ....
....
3. ....
....

...in my working life?

1. ....
....
2. ....
....
3. ....
....

Of my negative qualities, which is the one I would most like to change?
....
....

Having completed the above, don't destroy your answers. Keep them by you in order to prove (later) how much you have improved and how your self-esteem has permanently grown.

Internal conflict arises when you are not sure of yourself – in other words, when you are not sufficiently confident. Have you ever stopped to ask yourself *why* you are not as confident as you would like to be? Since no baby is born lacking in confidence, try asking yourself when you changed and in what way. Can you think of anything which might have occurred to make you feel less sure of yourself?

Natural confidence does not just disappear – something has to happen in order to make it do so. And one or more other people has to be involved. This does not mean that anyone was being deliberately unkind to you – although in some cases this may of course be true. Here a just a few examples of things which can destroy the confidence of someone very young:

A Sense of Rejection

When a marriage breaks up, unless the situation is handled very carefully a child will often assume that it is his (or her) fault. The parent who is leaving is rejecting *him*. And, since we are usually brought up to think that our parents are wise and wonderful people, it is natural for a child to feel that if such a person is rejecting him then there must be something very wrong with him.

It does not matter that, as this child grows up he will come to understand that marriages do break up and that it is not the fault of the children. The seed of the idea that he is not worthy of the love of his departing parent will have been sown and will continue to grow within him unless and until he makes a deliberate effort to do something about it.

While it is understandable that the child of a broken home could feel this way, many people do not realize that other forms of 'desertion' can have the same effect. If one parent dies – or even goes into hospital for a long time – a child will still experience it as a rejection and this feeling will remain with him – possibly buried deep in the subconscious – long after he is sufficiently adult for his logic to tell him that this absence was not undertaken on purpose.

Gillian was 18 months old in 1940 when her father went off to fight in the war. She had vague memories of this happy, laughing man who used to toss her in the air – and then suddenly and unexpectedly he was called up to fight in the war and, without explanation, he was gone from her life. Because Gillian was too young to understand what was happening, this situation alone could have caused her to have low self-esteem. But in her case, later events made it worse.

Four years later, when Gillian was five and a half, her father returned. By this time, of course, the little girl had grown accustomed to living just with her mother and to being the centre of her attention. Suddenly there was this great, tall man with a loud voice intruding on their lives and taking up so much of her mother's time – time that used to be given to her. Not only that but it was made clear that she was intended to love this big stranger – and that if she didn't she was being a naughty girl.

What a dilemma for her! Gillian wanted to please – but how could she suddenly love this man she did not even know? For her father, of course, the situation was quite different. During those four terrible years, one of the only things that had kept him going was the thought of returning to his beloved wife and daughter.

With some variation, this story was enacted in countless homes. Sometimes the father never came back; sometimes the child was so tiny that he or she had no memory of him at all. None of these things was the result of deliberate unkindness – after all, the men concerned had no choice in the matter – but in many, many cases it led to a deep sense of insecurity in the children of that time.

Being Made to Feel Inferior

There are many ways in which this can happen – some the result of deliberate action on someone's part and others the result of misconceived ideas.

One person – be it a parent, teacher or other figure of authority in a child's life – may be deliberately unkind. Even here, the type of unkindness may vary from scathing words to extreme punishment, from physical to sexual abuse. It is easy to understand how this can result in a child losing all confidence.

Sometimes, however, the person at fault may truly believe that he (or she) is doing what is best for the child. There are still those who think that the best way of 'persuading' someone to become a high achiever is to belittle every effort and criticize every result – in the hope of spurring that person on to greater things. But the devastating effect such treatment can have on a child who is anxious to please and who may genuinely be doing his best at the time can last well into adult life.

Disruption

This can cover many things and may only affect some children. While some might thrive, for example, on being sent to boarding school, others find it a truly distressing experience. Similarly, some children may be upset by repeated house moves, especially if each one means leaving friends and familiar surroundings far behind. If a child suffers repeated ill health or if a sibling dies, it can be sufficient to shake – and even shatter – a fragile self-image.

Changing Our Self-image

It is the inner image we form of ourselves in our very early years which remains with us unless and until we make a deliberate effort to change it. Of course it is quite possible to change our self-image, but there are two important points to bear in mind. First, many people do not believe that they can change themselves if they wish. 'It's just the way I am,' they say, 'I've always been like this.' Secondly, change takes effort.

As human beings, we are strangely resistant to change of any kind, and that includes change within ourselves. There seems to be a type of comfort in clinging on to what we already know –

even if what we know is not what we like. But the very fact that you are reading this book means that you want to improve the way you handle conflict – and if this involves making changes in yourself, you are already showing the sort of commitment which makes it likely that you will persevere and succeed.

Confident or not, we have all made mistakes in the past – and we are quite likely to make more in the future. The difference shows in the way in which the confident person regards his mistakes. While someone with a poor self-image may believe that his mistakes make him a failure in life, the person with a healthy self-image will look on them as part of the learning process of life.

If mistakes are those which can be put right, naturally the confident person will seek to do so. What he will not do is use them as a stick with which to beat himself for the remainder of his life.

Your attitude to your own errors shows in many ways. If you are confident, you will learn from them and do all you can to avoid repeating them. You will also be unafraid of tackling new problems, while the person who is not so confident will avoid them in case he gets it wrong again. Without your having to say a word, your attitude will show itself to others in your bearing and your body language, so they will easily become aware of your level of confidence. If you are trying to sort out a conflict between others and they realize that you are feeling less than confident about your ability to do so, you are unlikely to succeed.

Self-criticism

While it certainly pays to be honest with oneself, excessive self-criticism – particularly if not balanced by acknowledgement of self-worth – can cripple your confidence. Often it is an unwelcome echo of the way in which someone else criticized you all those years ago.

We all talk to ourselves – although often this conversation

takes place inside our heads. It is *the way* in which you do this which matters. It is so easy to think 'I wish I hadn't said that,' 'I came across so badly at that interview' or 'I wasn't really prepared for that meeting.' This is fine provided the inner conversation serves as a reminder to do better next time. But how often do we give ourselves any actual praise? When do we say to ourselves 'I carried that off rather well' or 'I did my very best at the interview'? Not often.

Most of us have been brought up to feel that it is wrong to be vain – and indeed that is the case. But it is not wrong genuinely to acknowledge that you have done something well. And, because we tend to build future progress upon past failures or successes, it is important to realize and be pleased about the fact of doing well.

Fear

Everyone but the most unfeeling individual feels afraid at some time, so accept that as natural too. It is what you do about that fear which matters. If you give in to it, you could allow it to rule your life. And you can be sure that, if you allow it to take over your thoughts, others will soon realize that you are afraid – whether dogs, potential muggers or those in your business over whom you are in charge.

The only thing to do about fear is to acknowledge that it exists – and then to act as if it doesn't. Remember the song in the musical *The King and I* which states 'For when I fool the people I fear, I fool myself as well.' Well, it works! When talking to salespeople, Dale Carnegie would say 'Act enthusiastic and you'll be enthusiastic.' I would say to anyone who has to deal with personnel situations and possible conflicts, 'Act unafraid and you'll be unafraid.'

Guilt

Guilt is another destroyer of confidence. We feel guilty about things we have done or things we have failed to do, things we have said or things we failed to say. But what good does this guilt do us? Of itself, it doesn't change a single thing. All it does is make us talk to ourselves in the most negative way possible.

In many cases guilt arises because of the views of other people – whether those we know (or knew in the past) or even so-called experts or the media who present an image of what should be, leaving anyone who does not conform to that image to feel that the fault must lie with him or her.

If you have a decision to make about future action, make it for yourself. Of course you may choose to seek advice from someone you respect – but you can also choose whether or not to act on that advice. What should be avoided is doing something which you instinctively feel is not right for you just because you feel you 'ought to'.

You may, of course, have a genuine reason for feeling guilty about something in the past. Perhaps you know perfectly well that you made a mistake in the way you handled a certain situation – but this does not make you a bad person. If such guilt exists, work through the following steps:

1) Acknowledge to yourself that you made a mistake.
2) If someone else is involved, and provided you can do so without causing him or her undue pain, acknowledge it to him or her too. Apologize if necessary and ask what you can do to put matters right.
3) Do whatever you can to rectify the situation. (Sometimes of course this is not possible – as in the case of a missed opportunity).
4) Decide what lessons you need to learn from the mistake so that it does not happen again – and therefore so you do not need to feel guilty about it again.
5) LET THE GUILT GO – IT HAS SERVED ITS PURPOSE.

Making Choices

Life consists of making choices. As soon as you are old enough to be able to think for yourself, you face one decision after another. Although naturally some of these choices are far more important and have far more effect on your life than others, none the less each is significant because it reinforces your ability to work towards your own current goal.

Having a goal at any time is also important. It doesn't matter whether it is a short- or long-term goal, as long as you have a direction in which to aim. It doesn't even matter if, halfway along that path, you decide that your original goal is not right for you and you wish to change direction. That doesn't mean that you were mistaken in your original aim but simply that, as you have grown and matured and come to know yourself better, you have decided that a different goal would be more appropriate for you.

At the beginning of this chapter you answered some questions. Look back now to the part where you wrote down what you considered to be your worst qualities and select any one of them that you would like to change. (A word of advice here – don't try to work on more than one at a time if you intend using the techniques I'm going to give you later in this chapter. It may seem like a good idea but will actually prove to be counter-productive.)

Now write down the aspect of yourself you wish to change and prop it up somewhere where you can see it. We'll come back to it very soon.

One of the most important choices you can make is to change some quality in yourself. And remember that, to be successful, it must be your choice alone. Never mind what other people think you should change – or even what you *think* they are thinking, which is not necessarily the same thing at all.

Changing yourself never succeeds in the long-term if it is done solely to please someone else. It could be that you decide to make the change because of the opinion of someone else whom you respect – but the final choice must still be yours.

Similarly, you cannot change others – only they are capable of doing it for themselves.

Many people are put off making changes because they think that it will be impossible or that it will be a hard and painful process. Neither of these is true. Yes, it will take effort on your part and, yes, it may be a little uncomfortable at first – but not for long. Psychologists consider that, provided the effort is sincere, permanent changes to personality traits can be made in as little as three to four weeks. If even that seems a little daunting, consider the alternative. There is an old saying that 'If you do what you've always done, you'll get what you have always got.' So, unless you are completely happy with your current situation, the only choice you can make if you are to live a more fulfilled life is to make those changes.

For the sake of clarity when it comes to working through the techniques, let's look at the following 'case study'.

William is a young man who has recently been promoted to team manager. He has always been a hardworking and conscientious individual – which is why the company have chosen to reward him with a promotion. But one of the areas where he is less confident than he would wish is in telling other people what to do. And yet he knows that this will form an integral part of his new job.

What are William's options?

- *He can approach other people quietly and cautiously and hope that they will do as he asks them.* Some will, of course. But there are always those who will take advantage of what they see to be weakness on the part of another human being. They will either ignore everything William says – almost challenging him to do something about it – or they may even make fun of him (either to his face or behind his back), thus completely undermining his authority both in the current situation and for the future.

- *He can bluff it out.* Whatever he may be feeling inside, William can act as though he is a confident person who is quite capable of handling staff. The trouble is that, however he may appear on the outside, in his own mind he will *know* that it is all an act and the anxiety he will feel about being found out at some point will make him, in fact, have an even less high opinion of himself.

- *He can choose to change*. This is the most sensible option because, even if it feels a little uncomfortable for a week or two, once William has made that change within himself it will be permanent – unless, of course, he deliberately decides to change himself once more to suit the situation which prevails at some future time.

If William chooses to change himself from someone who is nervous when issuing orders to others – particularly if they happen to be older than he is – to someone who is comfortable in an authoritative position, there will be cumulative after-effects. The first time he proves to himself that he can deal calmly and confidently with a situation which used to bother him, his self-esteem will grow and he will then be convinced that he can do something similar the next time – and he will. Now he will have two successes to build upon, and so he will find it becoming easier and easier to develop into the person he always wanted to be.

————————

Anger

Everyone feels some form of anger at some time, and only we ourselves know whether that anger is justified or whether we happen to be having a bad day when everything seems black.

Some people are afraid of their anger while others seem to thrive on it, throwing tantrums and indulging in other forms of negative behaviour. Neither extreme is satisfactory – the one because of the effect it has on you and the other because of the effect it has on those around you.

The important thing to realize is that anger is an energy and, as such, needs an outlet if it is not to do you harm. The best outlet, however, is not being aggressive towards other people as this achieves little apart from causing a considerable amount of bad feeling.

This does not mean that others should not know that you are angry – but do make sure that your anger is justified before stating it. It can often be far more effective to say quietly to someone 'That makes me really angry' than to shout and scream at them. Think about it: what is your natural reaction if someone yells at you? You are quite likely to shout back instinctively or to bluster and try to justify yourself. If you are very submissive you may become extremely distressed. None of these reactions is going to be productive when it comes to solving the problem which gave rise to the anger in the first place. But if you state quietly that you are angry, the other person will want to know why. This will start a conversation which at least stands some chance of either solving the problem or explaining how and why it arose.

Because anger is an energy, you should not deny its existence. Just find an alternative means of working it off. You may want to jog round the block, play a fast game of squash, dig the garden or just thump a cushion – any of these will serve the purpose and they won't create difficulties in relationships.

Analyse the Situation

Many of us go around acting and reacting without actually stopping to think about why we are behaving in a particular way – and whether it is the best way to achieve the results we desire.

Try to get into the habit of stopping from time to time to consider how you are feeling at that instant and what it is that has caused you to feel that way. The more you are able to understand yourself and your emotions, the more you will be able to build upon those aspects of yourself that you like while working to change those you do not. If you are to be able to manage other people when they are in conflict, the more understanding you have of what causes certain emotional reactions the better you will be able to do your job.

There may be times, for example, when you realize that you are not really reacting to the current situation but have carried forward your emotional response from something which happened earlier. If you react before you think, you can cause further damage to yourself and others – whereas if you stop and appreciate that such 'transposing' of earlier negativity is not fair, you are less likely to act on it. Not only will you feel better about yourself, but you will also have a deeper understanding of other people and what makes them react in the way they do.

Learn to Say No

This is something we all find difficult, whether in a work or personal situation. Of course, there are occasions – particularly at work – when someone in a senior position wants you to do something and it is almost impossible to refuse.

But the 'saying no' that I am referring to here is when we allow ourselves to be manipulated into doing something we really do not want to do – and where we have a choice.

Why is it that most people find it so difficult to say no? The predominant reason is that we all want to be liked and we feel that, if we refuse someone something – particularly when we have no apparently good reason for doing so – the person we have refused will not like us any more. But this is hardly ever the case – and, if it should happen, you can be sure that the person never really liked you in the first place.

It is also far better to refuse something than to go through with it and either do it badly or feel resentful about the whole matter. And, while you may choose to give a brief explanation for your refusal, don't feel that you have to make some long and involved excuse. A simple sentence will usually suffice. 'No, I can't take on any further commitments at the moment,' 'No, I don't like Indian food' or 'No, I have another engagement on that day.'

Optimism and Pessimism

Among the choices you can make about the way you want to change, you can decide which you want to be – an optimist or a pessimist. Now the same things may happen to these two people – but who is going to be happier?

Take a simple example. A husband and wife are planning a holiday in the sun. The husband, who is a pessimist, immediately begins to worry about possible delays at the airport, whether their luggage will arrive safely, if their house will be burgled while they are away, whether it will rain, what the hotel room will be like...and so on. By the time the holiday comes he will have had time to become thoroughly depressed.

His wife, however, is an optimist. As she contemplates their forthcoming vacation she imagines a scene of sun and sand, leisurely evening meals and dancing beneath the night sky. She gets far more than two weeks' enjoyment out of the holiday.

Now, whatever is going to happen on that holiday is going to happen to both the optimist and the pessimist. But one of them will already have had a miserable time while the other will have had a pleasurable one. Who would you rather be? Well, if you are not already an optimist, why not work at becoming one?

Techniques for Changing Your Life

Any or all of the following techniques work – all have been proved valid over a period of very many years and I have used them with my own clients, both individually and in group sessions, with excellent results. I would suggest that you give each a fair chance. Don't expect overnight miracles but, by using a combination of the techniques described, you should notice a definite difference within the space of two to three weeks. This should provide the impetus you need to keep going until the changes you have chosen to make become part of your very nature.

To make explaining the techniques simpler, I am going to use the example of the fictitious William who found it so difficult to tell other people what to do.

Preliminary Step: Relax!

Although it does not of itself solve your problems or make your changes, an essential first step is to learn how to relax properly. The better you are able to relax, the more easily you will be able to access your inner mind and make the changes you desire.

In this instance, relaxation does not mean flopping on a chair in front of the television set – or even having a good sleep. Relaxation is an art which can be learned and which will bring many benefits in addition to helping you make the changes you have chosen. You will feel better physically – your pulse rate and blood-pressure will be reduced and you will suffer less from excess stress.

You may feel that you would like to learn to relax with one of the many cassettes now on the market or by joining a relaxation class. But it is also possible to do so by following this simple routine.

Find a quiet, comfortable place where you will not be disturbed and sit or lie down comfortably. It does not matter whether you prefer a bed, a chair or the floor – but do try to make sure that your head and neck are supported in some way. Close your eyes.

Now, starting with your feet and working upwards through your body, tense and relax each set of muscles in turn (i.e. those in your toes, ankles, calves, thighs, abdomen, hands, arms, shoulders) until you come to those in your face, head, jaw and neck.

Next, spend a few moments establishing a slow and steady breathing rhythm. Actually take the time to *listen* to the rhythm of your breathing. And try to ensure that you breathe from your diaphragm rather than your upper chest.

Still with your eyes closed, create a picture in your imagination of a place that you would find beautiful. This can be a spot that you know or one which you invent – and of course it will be different for everyone. One person might like a cornfield while another prefers a beach; one might choose a country lane while another 'sees' a snowy mountainside. It doesn't matter what the image is, provided it is somewhere you would really love to be.

Spend ten minutes or so contemplating the beautiful spot you have created in your imagination. Get to know it; see it from every angle. Smell the scents, feel the textures, hear the sounds. The more real you can make this image, the more relaxed you will become.

Practise this routine daily until it becomes second nature to you and you are able to relax at will. Once you have reached that stage, you will be ready to proceed to changing yourself in the way you have chosen.

Step One

Think back through your life and remember a time when you really felt that you had succeeded at something. Before you say that you can't think of anything, it can be something which now appears quite trivial but which was a great achievement at the time. Perhaps when you first swam a width, played the piano with both hands or passed your driving test. When you have remembered some past accomplishment, spend some time thinking about the event and remembering just how it felt to be a success.

William chose the day he learned to ride a bicycle. Oh, the feeling of being free yet in control – the sensation of 'I've done it!'

Step Two

Now you need to harness the power of your imagination and visualize the successful outcome of the change you have decided to make.

Your imagination is an extremely powerful tool – in a positive or a negative way. We have all used it negatively at some time when we have contemplated the possibility of something going wrong – 'Suppose I forget my lines?', 'What if I drop it?', 'Perhaps I won't understand what they're asking me.' Anyone who has suffered from negative thoughts like these will know that thinking about something going wrong is almost enough to make it happen.

If negative use of the imagination works, then it follows that positive use must work too. So, go back to the change you have decided to make in yourself and create a mental 'home movie'. For example, William would imagine a scene in which he approached one of the more difficult members of his team and quietly and calmly issued the relevant instruction. He would see it in his mind as if it had already happened, observing his own positive demeanour and the satisfactory reaction of the person he was addressing. At the same time he would recall how he had felt when – all those years ago – he had successfully ridden his bicycle unaided for the first time.

The mind accepts the image of what has not yet happened, combines it with the remembered feeling of success and links the two. And, because your mind is so powerful, the two will always be linked so that, when you come to carry out the action in reality, not only will you act as a successful person, you will feel like one too.

This step needs to be repeated on a regular basis if it is to be effective. So try and set aside a little time – it need not be more than ten or fifteen minutes – every day for about two or three weeks. Then you will find that you can turn your created image into reality.

Step Three

Talk to yourself. No, it is not the first sign of madness but a highly effective means of motivating yourself. You have only to watch leading sportsmen and -women to see how much they talk to themselves when in competition. So, at regular intervals, remind yourself – preferably speaking the words aloud unless it would be embarrassing to do so – that you are a success, that you have chosen to make a change and that you have succeeded in doing so. William, for example, would tell himself 'I am capable of issuing instructions to people in a friendly but authoritative manner.'

Step Four

On small cards write statements which remind you of the success that you now are. You may choose to place these around you or you might keep them in a pocket to be brought out at intervals and looked at. The most important point about these 'affirmation cards' is that the statements written on them must read as though you have *already achieved* what you are setting out to do. In other words, one of William's cards would read: '*I am good at giving instructions*' (but not 'I am getting better at giving instructions').

You might wonder how simply reading these statements can be of assistance – and, indeed, alone they might not be enough. But combined with the relaxation, the remembered success and the visualization, they provide an extra boost. If you are doubtful about the validity of the written word, ask yourself why so many companies spend tens of thousands of pounds a year advertising their products. They put their words in newspapers, in magazines and on hoardings. Their images appear on television and in the cinema. If this combination of words and images did not convince the minds of the public of the value of their product, manufacturers would never bother to waste money on advertising, would they?

If you use the techniques described here, you will be able to make any change in yourself that you have chosen. (And then, of course, you can go back and work on the second negative quality, and then the third – and so on). The result will be that you will find yourself becoming more successful, more confident and with a greatly improved self-image. No longer will you need to be tormented by any form of inner conflict because now you will have the confidence to *know* what you think is right and to put it into action.

CHAPTER FOUR

Preventing Conflict

This book is about managing conflict but, of course, a great deal of conflict can be avoided if you take the trouble to select people who are most likely to be able to work well together. In this way, the only types of conflict likely to arise are those positive types we have talked about which can lead to new methods and ideas.

If a position becomes vacant in an existing team, you have the perfect opportunity to fill the gap with someone who you feel is likely to complement the existing members and work well with them. Advertising a position and then interviewing prospective candidates is a highly skilled and very efficient means of choosing the appropriate person to join the team.

It is not my intention to deal in this chapter with finding someone with the appropriate skills and knowledge to handle the practical requirements of the job in question. What we are concerned with here is to how to assess the personality of an interviewee and judge whether or not she (or he) would fit in well with the other members of an existing team.

What Are You Starting With?

If there is a position vacant, you first have to think about the members of the existing team – you should know them quite well by now but you might choose to take on board the opinion of someone else who works closely with them or comes into regular contact with them. It can be quite surprising to discover that someone else can hold a completely different opinion of others to the one you hold.

So, either alone or with a colleague, you must set about analysing the personalities of the present team. There are various questions about which you need to satisfy yourself. The most effective method is probably to create an analysis sheet for each individual member of the team.

What Are Their Positive and Negative Character Traits?

We all have our good and bad days but, if you know your team well, you should be well aware of each member's most dominant characteristics and the effect these tend to have on her (or his) colleagues.

Remember that you are considering these traits purely in regard to the working environment. Someone may be a charming chatterbox who might be well liked in a social situation but who, in the workplace, could drive colleagues demented by interrupting their train of thought with irrelevancies.

What Is Their Personality Type?

Are the various members of the team predominantly aggressive, submissive or assertive? Do they tend to be introverted or extroverted? Such considerations are important when bringing in a new member. It must be fairly obvious that it would not do to have too many aggressive people within one team – but a predominance of submissive people could prove to be just as disastrous. In an ideal world every company would be filled with assertive people. But, the world not being ideal, we can at least do as much as possible to keep the balance even.

Similarly, too many extroverts might make for a lively atmosphere but it could also be a highly stressful one, while a room full of introverts could be depressing and under-productive.

What Is the Business Hierarchy?

Is there a definite 'pecking order' or is everyone (in theory at any rate) of equal status although possibly doing different jobs? If there is an order of seniority, where exactly will the new person be expected to fit in and how will this be accepted by those already present?

Some companies have experienced great difficulty when a newcomer is placed in a position of seniority over existing team members. If this is what is to happen, it is important that the newcomer is chosen with great care and the situation explained clearly to her.

Knowing your existing staff, ask yourself how they are likely to accept a stranger joining the team. Are there any with whom you might need to have a quiet word first?

Are There Any Existing Personality Conflicts within the Team?

Look at the team as a whole and then at the member you are presently considering. If some sort of conflict already exists, ask yourself what part – if any – this person is playing in the situation. If she is, is it a helpful or obstructive one? Even if she appears to be standing on the sidelines, is she quietly encouraging discord on the part of someone else?

What Were the Past Personality Conflicts within the Team?

Every group of people will be in conflict at some point. Hopefully you will already have made note of any occasions when this has happened in the recent past, when most of the team members were the same as they are now. Taking each conflict separately, analyse with the benefit of hindsight how it came about, who was involved, whether it was quickly settled, who actually managed to deal with the problem and how she did so. This should tell you a good deal about the people already in your team and what type of newcomer would be most suitable.

Are They Good Communicators?

We shall be dealing with communication skills in detail in the next chapter, but you should be able to comment on each person you are analysing.

Does she explain herself clearly? Does she make sure others understand and then give them a chance to respond? Joining an existing group of any sort can be a daunting experience for any newcomer – but this made far worse if the individual members of that group cannot – or sometimes will not – help to instruct the newcomer in the ways of a particular organization.

Do They Prefer Working Alone or in Groups?

Even if everyone is working towards a common end, you will find those who prefer to shut themselves away and work on their own particular part of a job, only emerging to combine with other people when absolutely necessary. Others, however, thrive on tossing ideas backwards and forwards and discussing possibilities with as many like-minded people as they can. Where is your newcomer to fit in and with whom is she most likely to be working?

How Ambitious Are They?

While one person is quite happy to come in and do the job to her (or his) best ability without seeking advancement, public acknowledgement or promotion, to another these will be all-important. There is nothing wrong with being ambitious as long as this ambition does not become the be-all and end-all of life, making this person oblivious to the reality of situations around her. Introducing another ambitious person onto the scene might spur the existing team-member on to even greater achievements; on the other hand, she might see the newcomer is a rival to be beaten at every turn.

Once you have compiled and completed analysis sheets for each member of the existing team, you should be able to work out the type of person most likely to be suitable to join them. The size and type of organization are also important factors to consider. The needs and attitudes of people who work for a vast, international organization are likely to be very different to those of people who work for a small family concern.

Alison had been working her way steadily up the career ladder. Still in her late twenties, she had been doing extremely well in a large – if somewhat impersonal – organization. Her only reason for leaving was that her boyfriend had been offered an extremely good position with a company some 200 miles away and – knowing that she excelled at her work and that she would receive glowing references from her current employers – Alison had no doubt that she would soon find herself a suitable niche in their new home town.

As she had thought, she was offered the first job she went after. True, this was with a much smaller company than the one for which she had previously worked – but Alison rather liked the idea of being a very big fish in a smaller pool.

What Alison had not taken into account – nor had the manager who interviewed her – was that the atmosphere in a smaller, friendly team would be very different to what she had been used to. As far as Alison was concerned, she wanted to come in, do her job to the very best of her ability and then go home. She was not unpleasant to anyone but neither was she anxious to be over-friendly – possibly because she was accustomed to seeing everyone she worked with as a potential rival in the career stakes.

Her new colleagues were not used to such cool behaviour and immediately came to the conclusion that Alison was cold and aloof and considered herself above them. Naturally this did not endear her to them in any way at all, and the atmosphere in the office became stilted and uncomfortable where previously it had been warm and friendly. No one was disappointed when Alison was headhunted by a much larger organization and departed for better paid pastures new.

Selecting the right person to fit in with an existing team is important for everyone concerned – not only for those already working for the organization. A newcomer who does not feel comfortable with the other members will not be happy and will therefore not be likely to work to her (or his) full potential.

Attracting the Right People

Once you have decided the type of personality which would best complement your existing team, you have to set about letting the world know that this vacancy exists. It is up to you to decide whether to advertise directly yourself or to use an agency. Whichever you do, however, bear in mind that the actual wording of the advertisement is vitally important and can make all the difference between getting innumerable useless applications and attracting what you consider to be the best person.

Obviously your advertisement will give some indication of the type of work to be done and whether or not experience is needed, etc. But there are other points which should be incorporated – albeit subtly rather than blatantly:

- whether your company is a large one with perhaps a less personal leaning or whether it is a smaller family-type concern;
- whether the company policy is likely to be aggressive or friendly;
- the approximate size of the organization;
- whether it is exclusive or somewhat less up-market.

There is no point at all in 'dressing up' your company in order to make it seem something it is not. You will simply waste a great deal of time interviewing the wrong people. If you let it be known that you are one of the smaller, more friendly firms, you are probably not going to attract aggressively ambitious people like Alison. But, as we saw, you would not want to, as Alison's appointment did not work out well for anyone, and so wasted a great deal of everyone's time and efforts.

Application Forms

Once you have placed your advertisement you are likely – particularly given the job climate at the moment – to receive innumerable replies. Many of these are likely to come from people who are totally unsuitable for the position you are offering but who are desperate for work of some sort. You may feel compassion for such people, but the hard reality is that you cannot afford to waste your time – nor would it be fair to raise their hopes unnecessarily – by interviewing them.

This is where application forms come in. They help you to sort out those who are most likely to be suitable in order to offer them personal interviews.

There are ready-made application forms available which can be adapted for use in your particular organization – but, bearing in mind that you want to attract the right personality as well as someone who is able to do the job, it might well be better to create your own.

Naturally the application form you use will request all the usual information – name, address, etc. Also you will need to ask about the applicant's previous experience with the type of work you are offering. You will want to know where she (or he) worked before and her reasons for leaving her previous job.

In addition to all this, however, you will also need to know more about her as an individual and, although a CV might give you some of the answers you are seeking, the sections regarding personal life tend to call for very brief answers – often little more than a word or two.

Some of the additional requests you might make, therefore, are:

- asking the applicant to describe – as opposed to simply list – her hobbies and pastimes;

- finding out what her reasons are for wanting this particular job and why she thinks she has something special to offer;
- requesting a mini-autobiography giving information about her major life experiences.

Although CVs may be typewritten, you should always ask for the application forms – particularly the areas mentioned above – to be completed in the applicant's own handwriting. Not only does this give you the opportunity to take note of spelling, grammar, etc. and thereby gauge more accurately the level of her education, but, should you decide at any point to use the services of a graphologist specializing in recruitment, you will have ready-made examples of the necessary handwriting.

Once you have received the application forms, you will naturally need to sort through them, discarding those which are obviously inappropriate. Depending upon the number you have received, you may have to be even more selective as it simply would not be practical to interview dozens of people. So compare the personal characteristics indicated by the autobiographical sections of the form with the list of personality requirements you have already compiled. This will give you a better idea of which applicants you wish to see. You can then go about setting up interviews with them.

How to Get the Best Out of an Interview

Since, as the interviewer, you are the only person who knows precisely what you are looking for, it is essential to be well prepared in order to ensure that you do not omit anything important.

Obviously you will need to explain something about the company and define the job so that the applicant is well able to understand precisely what is required. But, bearing in mind that we are dealing primarily with personality here, there are several topics you might consider raising:

- Does the applicant tolerate/enjoy/actively seek personal responsibility or even authority?
- Does the applicant feel happier when there is a hierarchical 'reporting line' or when she can go straight to the top;
- What sort of person does the applicant consider:

  i would be capable of doing the job
  ii would enjoy doing the job
  iii would fit in best with the existing team?

- Is the applicant likely to react badly to any stress which might be involved in the job and, if so, how would she handle this?
- Is the applicant equally good at taking responsibility and doing what she is told, if and when the latter is appropriate?
- Does the applicant enjoy contact with the public – whether face to face or by telephone? In this case 'the public' might mean customers, clients or companies with whom your organization has dealings.
- How is the applicant likely to cope with the repetitive – and often comparatively boring – aspects of the job, such as form-filling, filing, etc. Does she appear to be sufficiently methodical to keep up to date with such tasks, even if she does not actively enjoy them?
- If one or more of the other team members is a highly-strung creative type, how likely is it that the applicant would be able to cope with this?
- Would the applicant take kindly to working under supervision should this prove to be necessary – particularly at the outset if new skills are to be acquired?
- Once she is familiar with the job, is the applicant willing to be innovative and try to come up with new ideas of her own?
- How good a communicator is the applicant – and therefore how likely is she to be able to put across her own ideas or express her own reservations?
- Is the applicant prepared to work to deadlines and, if so, is she likely to

  i keep to them and

   ii do so without being unduly adversely affected by the press-
     ure this is bound to create?

- Does it appear that the applicant is likely to co-operate well
  with others in the team or do you think she seems more
  inclined to want to get on only with her own aspects of the
  work?
- Do you think that the applicant is likely to be a useful member of the team when it comes to problem solving – or would
  she either become anxious or opt out of worrying about it
  altogether?
- Does the applicant appear to demonstrate a genuine enthusiasm, not only for the job on offer but for life in general?

You may well wish to add other areas of questioning for yourself but, provided you obtain a response to the questions above,
you are going to be better able to judge the personality of the
applicant and whether she is likely to fit in with the existing
team.

Of course, you do not have to ask all the above as direct questions. The idea is that they should be questions to which you
would like the answers, but direct interrogation is not always the
way. Provided you allow sufficient time for each interview and
provided your questions are sufficiently open, you should be
able to find the answers to what you want to know by paying
attention to what the applicant says in general conversation.

No one is going to be perfect and it is unlikely that you will
find someone whose every answer is just what you hoped to
hear – but, with these points in mind, you are probably going
to be able to sort out those applicants who are indeed most suitable for the job you are offering in every way.

Preparing for the Interview

It is important to prepare well for any interviews. Not only will
this allow you to remain calm and in control but it will help you

to concentrate on what the interviewee is saying. The more relaxed an atmosphere good preparation creates, the best possible chance the interviewees have to shine and to show what they are capable of. Naturally they will be nervous – and of course you'll make allowances for that – but they will be doubly on edge if they feel that you are uneasy about the whole situation.

Make sure the room in which the interviews are to be conducted is set out as you wish it. Ideally you do not want a room which is too austere and unwelcoming. A vast expanse of gleaming mahogany desk can be very daunting to someone who is already nervous. It also prevents good communication taking place – and since you really want to find the right person to fill the position available, good communication is essential. To sit behind a huge desk looking down on the unfortunate applicant may be a successful exercise in one-upmanship – but it rather defeats the object when you are trying to persuade interviewees to talk freely so that you can learn as much as possible about them.

My own opinion is that it is better not to have a desk or table between you at all. You will obviously need somewhere to put your papers and any printed information you wish to give the interviewee, but a low coffee table between two comfortable chairs should suffice. These chairs should face each other and be close enough to permit close communication but not so close that either of you feels that your personal space has been encroached upon.

If possible, try and sit sideways on to a window. It is extremely uncomfortable to stare towards bright light, and the one who is facing into the room with her (or his) back to the window might find that she is talking to someone whose face is completely in shadow – which does not encourage good communication.

When arranging your timetable for the day, be sure to leave a sufficient gap between each interview to allow you to make notes on the previous applicant. However well you think you will remember what each one has said and be able to distinguish clearly between them, by the time you have interviewed four or five you will not be able to do so.

You also need to use some of this time to read quickly

through the application form of the next interviewee and refresh your memory about what is written there.

Let it be known that you do not want to receive any telephone calls or interruptions of any sort while interviewing. It will do a great disservice to someone who could possibly be an excellent employee and it will make it extremely difficult for you to maintain sufficient concentration.

Prepare a sheet with some points on it which you feel are of special significance; you can then tick these or not as the interview progresses. There is nothing wrong with making a few *brief* notes during the course of the interview – indeed it indicates that you are taking the interviewee seriously and listening to what she is saying. But the notes should not be copious as the interviewee might then be tempted to slow down and wait for you to catch up and thus would not be speaking spontaneously. In addition, while you are concentrating on what you are writing you cannot be paying sufficient attention to what is being said.

Do make allowance for some nervousness on the part of the interviewee – it's only natural. In fact, I would be more concerned if the person I was talking to did not display any anxiety whatsoever. This type of nervousness is not an indication of the permanent state of the candidate and, if you can allow the interview to continue long enough to enable her to relax and talk naturally, you will gather a far better impression of her type of personality and be able to compare it with the one you are seeking.

If you spend a few moments introducing yourself and then indulging in small talk, the candidate should be able to relax more easily. When it comes to the part where she is talking about hobbies and interests, you should be better able to judge her personality by what she says, how she says it and by her body language.

THE EIGHT-POINT INTERVIEW

1) Introduction and small talk. This gives you both an initial breathing space – the candidate because she is able to relax and not feel that she is being interrogated, and you because you simply have to take the time out to introduce yourself

and get settled down before the interview begins in earnest.

2) Talk about the job in more detail, explaining precisely what will be expected, what the responsibilities and possible obstacles may be, the salary, hours, etc.

3) Referring to the completed application form, discuss the candidate's abilities in the required areas. You can also ask at this point about previous experience, the reasons for wanting this particular job and the reasons for leaving the last one. If qualifications are important, then this is the point at which they should be established.

You will see that, until this point, you have done most of the talking, which should allow the candidate to relax more and more and see you as a human being rather than just 'an interviewer'. When she does have to reply, it will be with information with which she is perfectly familiar and which concern matters of fact – so there is no sense of being 'put on the spot'.

4) Ask the candidate if there are any questions about the position being offered – or indeed about the company itself. By the time you have answered these, you will have established good communication between the two of you and will be ready to lead on to other topics.

5) This is the point at which you should begin to get the candidate to talk about her own interests. She should be sufficiently relaxed in your company by now to talk freely and without restriction. Watch for signs of genuine enthusiasm in both verbal and non-verbal language.

6) Now that the candidate is as at ease as she is likely to be during the course of the interview, it is time to introduce into the proceedings any form of questionnaire or test you might feel would be helpful, being certain to explain any instructions fully to the candidate at the time.

7) To relieve the stress of having to complete a test (if there has been one), allow just a few moments of general discussion. This can cover anything from small talk to any extra questions either of you might wish to ask.

8) Now it is time to bring the interview to a close. You must take the lead in this by rising to your feet and extending your hand for a handshake. Whatever you have thought about the candidate, be pleasant. Even if she is completely unsuitable, there is no point in hurting her feelings unnecessarily.

As a matter of courtesy, each candidate should be given an approximate idea of when she is likely to be informed about the outcome of the interview. Having given her a date, it is up to you to keep to it insofar as it is at all possible.

Immediately afterwards, take time to make some notes – preferably on a ready-prepared sheet. It is also helpful to place the candidate on a scale of 1 to 5 – 1 being totally unsuitable and 5 indicating that she is well worth considering.

Useful Techniques

The following suggestions may prove helpful – particularly if you are attempting to establish the personality of interviewees and decide whether or not they will fit in well with members of your existing team.

Open Questions

If you want to encourage candidates to talk so that you have the opportunity not only to listen to what they say but to observe their body language, you will have to ask open questions. Open questions are those to which it is not possible to give a simple 'yes', 'no' or other one-word answer.

Closed questions are those which do have this basic monosyllabic answer, i.e. 'How long did you work for Smith & Co.?' Answer – 'Ten years.' 'Do you enjoy driving?' Answer – 'Yes.' This type of question has its place, such as when you require a specific piece of information.

An open question, however, requires elaboration. For

example: 'What is your opinion of...?' 'What do you feel about ...?'

Multiple Questions

Multiple questions are a number of queries strung together in one long sentence. For example: 'Tell me about the type of work you were doing for Smith & Co. – I expect the set up was quite different to the one you found when you were with Brown Ltd; did they have as many employees as Smiths, or as big a share of the export market?'

Multiple questions are rather a waste of time, as all that will happen is that the interviewee will answer the last of the series – or perhaps the easiest one.

Leading Questions

If you are trying to learn more about the personality of interviewees, leading questions should also be avoided. A leading question is one where you turn what is really a statement into a question. For example, 'So if you do come and work here, you would be quite prepared to fit in with the rota system I've described?' What is the candidate to say but 'yes'? If she disagrees with you, not only does she sound churlish – but she knows she probably won't get the job!

Hypothetical Questions

These can be extremely useful when you want others to open up to you so that you can assess their personality. If you ask questions which begin, 'Tell me about...' , 'What would you do if ...?' or 'Suppose you were to...?', the interviewee has no alternative but to talk to you.

Body Language

We shall be looking at this in more detail in the next chapter, but some basic points to consider are:

- Does the candidate maintain reasonable eye contact with you? You would not want her (or him) to stare fixedly into your eyes the entire time – that would be extremely unnerving and an indication of something wrong – but neither should she go out of her way to avoid your glance altogether.
- Does she keep her arms folded across her chest? Of course this could indicate that she is feeling cold – but it is more likely to mean that she is trying to avoid being drawn into saying too much and is determined to keep her distance.
- Is her posture such that she tends to keep leaning away from you? This is another way of indicating that she is doing all she can to keep a distance between you. It may mean that she has already made up her mind that this job is not for her, or that she does not want to give away too much about herself.

Language, Dress, etc.

Do you feel that the candidate's vocabulary indicates an unsuitability for the position for which you are considering her? It is not wise, in an interview situation, to place too much reliance on the candidate's tone of voice, because this can so easily be affected by nervousness. But you may be tempted to reconsider if her vocabulary tends to indicate an insufficient educational standard or if her language is coarser than you would like – particularly bearing in mind that most people try to be at their best during an interview.

Whether the interviewee's mode of dress bothers you or not is a purely personal response – and much depends upon the type of job on offer. You would not expect a prospective City accountant to be wearing the same as someone seeking a position in a flourishing public relations and advertising agency.

However, what you are entitled to expect is that the candidate has chosen to wear clothes in keeping with the position she is seeking.

Other Aids

Psychological and Psychometric Tests

These tests come and go as the mood of the times dictate. Some individuals and some organizations place far greater reliance upon them than others. Indeed some companies *insist* that everyone should take some form of psychological or psychometric test before being accepted.

They can certainly be helpful in some ways, but they can never be the entire answer because there are certain points to bear in mind:

- A test is useless if it is obvious that there is a 'correct' answer to each question, as candidates are likely to opt for that one, whether or not it would be their genuine response. The only tests of this sort which are valid are those to which any of the answers would appear to be positive and so the candidates do not feel inhibited about choosing the one which truly reflects their opinion.
- Some people, particularly if they have applied for several jobs recently, have become so accustomed to completing these tests that it does not really give a true indication of their abilities. This applies particularly in the case of those psychological tests which ask you to state the next number in a sequence or to select the odd one out in a series of diagrams.
- The way in which the tests are completed can be greatly influenced by the fact that the candidate is nervous – even though you may have done what you could to put her at ease before thrusting the test at her.

So use these tests if you wish, but consider them only as

additional aids when it comes to making your final decision. They do give an indication of intelligence, speed of thinking and also – in the case of psychometric testing – personality and aptitude, but they should not be the only thing taken into consideration.

Graphology

An increasing number of organizations are employing the services of a professional graphologist at the recruitment stage. The handwriting of the applicant is considered in great detail and a good graphologist will be able to tell you a considerable amount about the personality of the individual concerned.

Once again, it is up to you whether or not to employ such techniques. Without doubt graphology can be a useful additional tool when it comes to making your selection – particularly when it is someone's personality you are considering.

Contrary to what many people think, the graphologist will require far more than the applicant's signature. Indeed, an entire page of handwriting is preferred if possible. This is the reason behind asking for the application form – and particularly the autobiographical section – to be completed in the applicant's own handwriting.

After the Interviews

If, even after studying your own notes as well as the results of any tests or graphological examination, you are still unsure about which candidate to employ, don't hesitate to call back the most likely ones for a second interview. It will take up more of your time, but if you do not choose the right person this time, you might find yourself having to repeat the entire process in the near future – and that would take up even more time.

Listen to your intuition. If a particular applicant seemed perfect on paper, answered all your questions well and passed the relevant tests – and yet some gut instinct tells you that you should not employ her, I would suggest you pay attention to it.

Intuition or instinct should certainly not be the only consideration, but if you have worked with people for some time and something warns you against a particular individual, I believe you should take notice of that. After all, you will have to work with her too.

If you plan and conduct your interview well, not only should you find the candidate who is going to be most able when it comes to doing the job, but you will find the one who has the right personality to mix well with existing members of your team. If you have chosen well, you will find yourself having to deal with far less negative conflict in the future.

CHAPTER FIVE

Good Communication

Good communication is obviously a vital ingredient in the successful running of any aspect of your life. You could be the most caring person in the world, have truly innovative ideas, be the most knowledgeable on a particular subject – but if you are not able to communicate, all these gifts will be to no avail.

Nowhere is the lack of good and effective communication more keenly felt than in the workplace. As Jane Allan writes in her book *How to Solve Your People Problems*:

> *Communication failure is one of the greatest management problems in the UK today, mainly because people realise neither the importance of getting it right nor the difficulties in the art of effective communication.*

Many conflict situations at work could probably be avoided altogether if only people knew the best way to communicate with each other. Some people only half-say what they want to convey. Others only half-listen or, if they have listened properly, only half-understand what has been said. Yet others react to what they *think* the other person has been trying to say.

It is worth taking the time to establish principles of good communication among those who work with or for you if conflicts are to be avoided. If you do not feel able to do this yourself, the expense of calling in a professional trainer to run a short (possibly only one-day) course in Communication Skills will be more than amply repaid because of the reduction in time-consuming misunderstandings and conflicts.

Because all but a few of us are born with the inherent ability to speak and hear, we tend to take communication skills for granted and so we do little to learn about or improve them. It is only those who have the misfortune to be deficient in one of these skills who truly appreciate the value of the skills they *have* got and actively work at enhancing them.

A manager who takes the time and trouble to develop his (or her) skills as an observer and a listener will have the ability to see conflict coming and to nip it in the bud before it becomes serious, thus possibly avoiding what could be massive problems in the workplace.

Written Communication

Written communication is seldom sufficient when used alone because:

- It does not allow the recipient to clarify any points of which he might be unsure.
- There is no opportunity for questions to be asked.
- Many people either put a written document to one side to be read 'later' (only later never comes or the document itself is lost) or they 'speed-read' it, possibly missing or failing to understand fully some relevant point.
- It is possible – as any student will tell you – genuinely to read every single word of a chapter or a document without ever absorbing the meaning of what is written there.
- Even when a document is 'properly' read, we only take in a relatively small percentage of what is written or printed there.

If a situation is one which obviously calls for written communication, it should form only part of the whole. Verbal communication should be used – either in advance or after the written document – to ensure that all points have been fully understood by everyone.

Even at meetings where written communications may be handed round, it is a good idea to ask for verbal reports in order to focus everyone's attention on the salient points.

Spoken Communication

Because it is so important, in this chapter we are going to concentrate predominantly on spoken communication.

What are the processes when one person wants to say something to another?

A wants to say something to *B*. First he thinks about what it will be and then he says the words. But suppose *A* is talking about something of which he has a greater understanding than *B* – he might well speak too quickly, too quietly or even leave out some relevant points because to him they are obvious. If that is the case, *B* will not receive the correct message and, if she says nothing, *A* will go off thinking that he has successfully conveyed his meaning.

Of course, *B* has a choice to make. She can remain silent or she can make it clear that – for whatever reason – she has not fully understood what *A* was trying to say. The choice she makes will depend greatly on her personality and her feelings about *A*. Perhaps *B* is an anxious person or perhaps she is rather afraid of *A* – she may say nothing. Then, when she either does not do as asked or when she does something but it is wrong, *A* may become angry. *B* will try to justify herself. Result – conflict.

However, if *B* does point out to *A* that she has not fully understood what was said, the latter may become impatient and even aggressive. *B* may then either bluster or become aggressive herself. Result – conflict.

If you find yourself in the position of needing to pass on a message, to give information or to make an explanation, *always* allow the listener an opportunity to give feedback. This will give him the opportunity to ask questions or indicate if he has not fully understood. If all is well and the message has been perfectly received, he should be able to prove this by paraphrasing back to you what you have told him. In this way, both of you will know what is expected and how you feel about it.

'Paraphrasing' is the important word here. Nothing is proved if the listener simply repeats your own phrases, word for word. It is quite possible to do that without having understood the meaning behind the message. But to give the same message in one's own words indicates that one has properly understood what has been said.

Communication through a third party is rarely successful. Most of us, when little, played the game called 'Chinese whispers' (known also as 'Telephone' in some parts of the world), when a simple message was passed down the line from person to person. It rarely if ever was the same message when it reached the end of the line as when it had first been uttered.

Some organizations are so concerned with status and hierarchy that they insist that information is passed down in this way. If you are involved in such an organization, you must be sure to follow up the verbal message with confirmation in writing. In this way no one will have an excuse for misunderstanding what he has been told and each will have an opportunity to seek further clarification if he is not certain what was meant.

If you have some information which has to be given to several different people, the best way to go about it is to tell them all together so that they all hear the same thing at the same time. This should also give them an opportunity to ask questions and to discuss the matter.

Difficulties

There are various problems which can cause a breakdown in communication even in what seems to be the simplest transfer of information between *A* and *B*.

- Each of us is influenced by our own beliefs, fears, prejudices, etc., so we all see and understand things differently. Before he even opens his mouth, the words *A* formulates inside his head will reflect this.
- The existing relationship between *A* and *B* will affect both the

speaker and the listener. Are they on equal footing or is one in a superior position to the other – and, if so, which one? What do they feel for each other – fear, respect, affection, contempt...? Imagine how you would feel to be given a piece of information, first by someone you like and respect and then by someone for whom you feel contempt. The way you would receive that information would be very different in each case.

- The time and place of the conversation can also affect the communication process. If *A* is attempting to pass on a piece of information immediately before attending an important meeting or just before leaving to go home, he is less likely to pay attention to whether or not *B* has fully understood what he is saying. On the other hand, if it is not information being passed on but a criticism being made, the spot where this takes place can make a significant difference. If it occurs in a public place, *B* may be so embarrassed and so anxious that no one overhears what is being said, that she fails to register the actual words being spoken. Even if no one else is present, if *B* thinks there is a chance that someone might appear on the scene, the result will be the same.

- The state of health and fitness of either *A* or *B* can also have an effect on the success of the communication. If *A* has a headache, for example, he will want to get the whole thing over with as quickly as possible and so may not take the time and trouble to explain things as well as he otherwise might. If *B* is standing during the conversation and she happens to have a bad back, she might be so anxious to get away and sit down that she agrees to what is said without really thinking about it or fails to give appropriate feedback if there is something she does not understand.

- External interruptions affect some people more than others. General noise may not bother one person at all while it may completely destroy the concentration of the other. Other people interrupting or the telephone ringing will break the train of thought of both speaker and listener.

- The actual language used can sometimes prove to be a barrier – not only if the speaker and the listener come from different national backgrounds or have different standards of education. Sometimes technical words are used which are completely familiar to the speaker but which the listener either does not understand or needs more time to absorb and assimilate with what he already knows.

- Similarly, and particularly if A is in a senior position to B and attempting to give her instruction, A may think that B already has a greater level of knowledge than she actually has. This can cause A to use terminology which is over B's head, or to give the instruction too rapidly. If A does not then stop to seek feedback so that he knows B has grasped his meaning, the whole thing may prove to be a wasted exercise.

- Many people nowadays suffer from stress in their place of work and this stress can cause physical reactions in the body which make it more difficult to take in new information. If you are suffering from stress, you are more likely to be angry or anxious and this can prevent you functioning effectively. You will therefore not be a good speaker or a good listener. Pressure at work (or problems at home) may be so great that you find it difficult to concentrate on what is being said.

- If A tries to send a long message to B without taking a break – and particularly if it is delivered in a monotonous tone of voice – B will lose concentration and her mind will begin to wander off on to other subjects. Anyone who has ever attended a lecture or a speech where the orator has talked for a considerable length of time without breaking up the talk with visual aids, jokes, group activities, etc., will know just how easy it is for the mind to leave the topic being discussed and roam through any number of other subjects.

- Not only might A and B be affected by their own emotions, but a breakdown in communication can arise because one or both of them is so insensitive that he (or she) does not appreciate the emotional state of the other. If A has just had a row at home, he may well appear to be more brusque than normal; if B is in awe of A or is upset because she has just been hauled over the coals by the boss, she is going to be extremely nervous. Even if the cause of the emotional state is

not known, it is up to both *A* and *B* to b
other.

- Different personal backgrounds may give *A*
starting point. To someone who owns a ma
and a yacht, a holiday in the Bahamas may app
to the young couple struggling to bring up t
a relatively low income, the same holiday   be an
extravagance not even to be considered. To someone who has
worked in a particular industry for 20 years, a particular task
may appear simple, while to the young person who has only
been with the company for six weeks that same task would
seem extremely difficult.

AIDS TO EFFECTIVE COMMUNICATION

- Listen actively. This means doing more than just 'hearing' the
words being spoken. If you can turn them into pictures in
your head at the same time, you will be more likely to focus
on the true meaning of what is being said – and it will be
more likely to fix itself in your mind.
- It may sound pedantic – but stand or sit straight and breathe
deeply. This allows more oxygen to travel to the brain, thus
keeping you more alert while the other person is speaking. A
straight back and deep breathing also work particularly well if
you are feeling tired or bored.
- Observe the body language of the speaker. In this way you are
likely to take in more than is said by the actual words spoken.
Use your judgement here, though, and don't allow yourself
to rely on a single example of the speaker's body language.
Discomfort or a habitual mannerism may appear to demonstrate a negative body language signal – but only place real
importance on it if you can see two or three things all of
which lead you to the same conclusion.
- Try to develop an interest in what the other person is actually saying. Sometimes this will be easy; at others not. You
can make it come more naturally by attempting to formulate
mental questions as he (or she) speaks.
- If there is something about which you are not quite clear,

e to ask for further information at the first possible
portunity. For any new knowledge to make sense, it has to
be added to what we already know. If you fail to understand
something at a quite basic level, you will never be able to add
further information to such a shaky foundation.

If you are the communicator, make sure that you get feedback
at regular intervals – it really is important. And be certain that it
is the right type of feedback. There is no point in asking someone 'Do you understand?' – because he is almost bound to say
yes. Listeners need to be able to put what you have said into
their own words to prove that they have fully understood it.

As the communicator, if there is anything of importance you
wish to say, it helps to work out in advance the 'Who...what...
when...where...why?' of the situation to ensure that you can
make best use of your opportunity to give information.

Who?

With whom are you about to communicate, and what is the
existing state of his (or her) knowledge? Will you be speaking
to more than one person and, if so, will they be starting from
different levels of expertise and experience? If this is the case,
you need to find a way to pass on the additional basic information to those who know least while maintaining the interest level
of those who have greater knowledge.

What?

What do you want to say? This may appear to be a ridiculous
question, but anything of significance needs to be worked out
in advance in the same way that you would work out a speech
or presentation – even though what you have to say may be
shorter than either and addressed to only one person.

So, just as if it were a presentation, you need to have a beginning, middle and end to your communication – making sure, of
course, that you allow ample time for feedback, whether in the

form of paraphrasing or of questions.

When?

When do you wish this communication to take place? If it is some sort of instruction or explanation, obviously it needs to be said before the listener actually begins working on the particular project in question.

If it is something important you wish to say, timing can be vital. Don't begin a lengthy explanation five minutes before leaving time or when the listener is in the middle of an important task for someone else. Equally, if you are doing your best to settle a conflict or reassure someone who is feeling anxious, you will want to take the first available opportunity in order to put minds at rest as soon as possible.

Where?

Where should you speak? You want to be able to hold your listener's attention – and one of the ways of accomplishing this is to maintain eye contact. This is not so easy to do if you are both striding along a corridor or across the car park. The more important the words you have to say, the more essential it is to find a spot where complete concentration is possible – away from possible interruptions and the general hustle and bustle of a busy work environment. A quiet office, an empty room – these are likely to suit your purpose best. In some cases – particularly when dealing with one person whose behaviour is the cause of some friction or conflict – it can be advantageous to get him away from the 'battle zone' altogether. A trip to a local coffee shop at a quiet time of day can often work wonders.

If what you have to say is in any way critical of one or more people, make sure that you speak to them alone. There is never justification for belittling someone in front of other people – the humiliation he would experience will be more likely to increase the amount of conflict rather than reduce it.

If two or more people are involved in the conflict, it can be very helpful to speak to them at the same time and to ask them to put their own points of view to you calmly and quietly in front of the other(s) involved. This is a method frequently used by counsellors of all types, and ensures that the friction and raised tempers often caused by direct confrontation between the parties are avoided. It will be your job to remain calm and in control throughout and to allow each person ample time to speak while insisting that he (or she) does so in a reasonable and positive manner.

Why?

Why is this communication necessary in the first place? This may seem another obvious question, but actually sitting down and thinking about your reasons may help you to ensure that you cover all the relevant points.

It can be helpful to bear in mind that when a verbal communication takes place, various processes are involved:

What *A* thinks he is saying

What *A* actually says

What *B* thinks she hears

What *B* really hears

What *B* thinks she replies

What *B* actually replies

What *A* really hears

What *A* thinks he hears.

Although *A* and *B* may only say one sentence each, all of these processes will be gone through. If the communication has been effective, there will be no difference between what an individual *thinks* he hears and what he *actually* hears. But there is no way of knowing whether the communication is effective without checking. So we are back, once again, to the importance of feedback.

Naturally, if you are *A*, you will find some way of couching your request for feedback in non-confrontational terms. You do not want to sound boorish or dominating, so you could say to *B* that you would like him to tell you, in his own words, what you have just said and that your reason for wanting this is to ensure that you have put it across well. Depending upon his feedback, you will soon discover if you are a good communicator or if there is room for improvement.

It is best to seek feedback at an early stage during a long explanation. In this way you will discover whether you are managing to make clear what you are saying. And, if instructions or explanations are involved, you will want to know at the earliest possible moment whether there is some lack of understanding on the part of your listener. In this way you will not build misapprehension upon misapprehension, thus compounding what might have been a very minor failure to understand a small basic point.

Equally you need to give your own feedback at an early stage. Suppose someone does something quite minor which happens to annoy you; you may decide that it would be petty to mention it and so you let it pass. What happens then? The person who has been annoying you is quite unaware of having done so and therefore has no reason to stop what he has been doing. Your annoyance will continue to escalate as he continues until you explode with rage at him, while he has possibly no idea at all of what he has done that is wrong. Many conflicts begin in just such a way.

Had you made a quiet comment at the outset, however, it is unlikely that offence would have been taken and the situation would have come to an end before it could become confrontational.

Sometimes it is necessary to give directional feedback; to do this you must remain assertive. 'Let's get back to the point' is one way of expressing in an assertive (though not aggressive) way what it is you need from the speaker.

Feedback can also take the form of either a compliment or criticism; both of these take practice if you are to give and receive them well.

Compliments

Many people are loathe to pay compliments, finding it embarrassing to do so – and indeed nothing sounds worse than obviously false praise. But a genuine compliment, honestly paid, can do so much to boost morale and encourage loyalty.

Everyone likes to feel that he (or she) is appreciated, and sometimes a few simple words are all that is required. (This is one of the instances when, of course, it is quite all right to make a comment in front of other people – provided you are careful to ensure that the compliment paid to one does not imply criticism of the others).

Don't be disheartened if your listener finds it difficult to respond properly to a sincere compliment – this is a common failing, particularly in Britain where it seems to be the norm to put oneself down. How many times have we all heard a negative response to a compliment?

'I do like your outfit'…'What, this old thing? I've had it for ages.'

'That was a very thorough piece of work'…'Oh, I just did the first thing I thought of.'

If you are ever in the pleasant position of having a compliment paid to you and you cannot think of an appropriate reply, remember that a simple 'thank you' is all that is needed. To come back with a negative response is really an insult to the person paying the compliment; it is like saying that his opinion is worth nothing.

Criticism

There may be times when it is necessary to express your criticism of one or more individuals, and there are some points to bear in mind here:

- All spoken criticism should have a purpose and not be a way for the critic to relieve his (or her) own feelings;

- *Never* voice criticism of one person in front of others. Find a way of taking him to one side so that you do not cause him humiliation. If you are dealing with someone whom it is very difficult to pin down, it may be worth 'making an appointment' with him – 'I can see you're busy right now, but I'd like to have a word with you; how about two o'clock in my office?'
- Limit your criticism to what is justified, avoiding what is judgemental. 'This is the third time you have made a mistake in a piece of research' is valid (if true) – but going on to say 'you're stupid' or 'you're lazy' is not, as such comments are judgements and not criticisms.
- Sometimes there is a better way of going about things than being openly critical. Take the time to consider other methods before voicing your criticism. If you come to the conclusion, however, that a critical comment is essential, remain assertive – which means that there is no need to shout or act aggressively. Statements of fact, put forward in a quiet voice, are actually far more effective than yelling at someone. Such an attitude will probably lead to some sort of shouting match during which both parties are likely to lose control and say things – often causing irreparable damage – which they later regret.
- If you find yourself in the position of having to respond to someone else's criticism of you, bear in mind that you should only respond to that part which is critical and not that which is judgemental or exaggerated.

Judgemental Language
'You've got the method wrong again – you're absolutely useless.' The first part may be true but the last part is judgemental and you can ignore it in your response.

Exaggeration
'You're ten minutes late! You're always late!' You may be ten minutes late but it is unlikely that you are *always* late – or you would have heard about it before now!

Whatever the criticism, if it is valid all you can do is reply to the part which is true, apologize if appropriate, say what you are going to do about it, and carry out your promise. For example:

'Yes, I am late. I'm sorry. I'll stay ten minutes later this evening and I'll do my best not to let it happen again.'

Giving Verbal Information

When it comes to a meeting where information is to be passed on, you have various choices:

- a meeting of full staff
- a meeting of individual sections, one at a time
- a one-to-one meeting with an individual.

A meeting must be the right size for the type of information you wish to communicate:

- If it is something which is going to affect everybody, make sure you tell them all at the same time. Remember that the grapevine can pass on information more quickly – although often less accurately – than you. So don't give it a chance to flourish.
- If the information is going to affect different sections or different teams in different ways, tell them one at a time. This will give you an opportunity to concentrate on those points which are most relevant to the particular individuals concerned and to get the appropriate feedback from them.
- If only one person is really going to be affected, tell that person at a one-to-one meeting.
- If the information affects everybody to some extent but one individual predominantly, tell that person first and then call a full meeting in order to tell the others.
- Except when you know only one person is involved, if you have any doubts about how many people to tell at once, it is better to tell too many rather than too few. In this way you will avoid rumours and mistaken reporting of what you have

been saying.
- If you have to handle a conflict situation between, say, two members of your team, talk to them together so that there can be no doubt about what is being said – both by you and by each of them. Ask each in turn what he (or she) thinks is the cause of the problem between them, giving each of them plenty of time in which to reply. And, to save tempers flaring, each should address his answer to *you* and not to the person with whom he is in conflict.

When each has had a chance to put his own point of view, ask each of them what he thought when he heard the other person's version. Did it accord with his own? If not, in what way did it differ? How does each think it arose that there were two different versions of a single problem?

Once they have sorted out their differences (if any – but there will be) with regard to the actual situation, ask each of them in turn to suggest a possible solution – once again giving them ample time to speak. (Time spent on this meeting will be well spent, as it may bring the conflict to an end, thus benefiting both individuals and the company).

If their solutions do not tally precisely, ask them whether they are prepared to reach a state of compromise and, if so, in what way. Unless one or both of them is particularly unreasonable – in which case you may well decide that you do not want them in your team – a compromise will usually be agreed upon and the problem solved.

Unless important rules are being broken – in which case, of course, you will have to point this out and state what you intend to do about it – try to avoid telling them what to do. They are far more likely to agree upon and stick to a compromise they decide upon for themselves.

Body Language

It is said that, during the course of communication we gain 7 per cent of our information from the actual words being used,

13 per cent from the tone of voice of the speaker and a massive *80 per cent* from his (or her) body language.

Body language can reinforce verbal communication by:

- backing up what we are saying – when, for example, you maintain a demonstrably assertive stance while saying 'I am absolutely determined that we will succeed.'
- letting others become aware of our state of mind – so that they can tell by your expression and/or your posture that you are happy/anxious/exhausted, etc.
- replacing verbal communication altogether – as in a shrug of the shoulders when you don't know an answer or a shake of the head when you wish to say no.

But body language can also cause problems:

- It can contradict what we are saying – when, for example someone replies to your query with 'I'm fine' while his body language is such that his obviously is not.
- It can be misleading – as when you send mixed signals by saying how pleased you are about something while maintaining a 'closed' body language (arms folded across chest, posture rigid, avoiding eye contact).
- It can be so misleading that those observing do not get any message at all.

Positive Body Language	Negative Body Language
Looking at the other person's face	Avoiding looking at the other person at all
Making frequent eye contact	Avoiding the other person's eyes or staring aggressively
Nodding and smiling as the other person speaks	Repeatedly licking your lips or clearing your throat
Uncrossing your arms	Keeping your arms folded

Having 'open' hands	Clasping your hands tightly together
Steepling your fingers	Banging the table or pointing at the other person
If standing, turning towards the other person	Standing over someone who is seated
Sitting with your legs uncrossed	Sitting with your legs crossed – particularly if you swing one leg
Leaning slightly towards the other person	Leaning away from the other person
Sitting when the other person sits, standing when the other person stands	Striding around the room disregarding the other person's body language
Maintaining a relaxed posture	Fidgeting

Now you might say that you always cross your legs when you sit or that you are in the habit of folding your arms across your chest, but that you are really a warm, friendly and assertive person. That might well be so – but what we are looking at here is the message you are *actually* sending as opposed to the one you *intend* to send. If all your other body language is positive but you happen to have your legs crossed, I don't suppose that anyone will misread you. But should you demonstrate, even unwittingly, two or more negative body language traits at the same time, you are in danger of being misunderstood.

Remember that, where there is a conflict between the spoken word and body language, it has been shown that most people will respond more to the body language.

For this reason, if you are the person receiving the message bear in mind that a single negative body language trait may mean nothing at all. After all, someone who is getting over a cold may clear his throat frequently – even though in many other cases this could be a sign of nervousness. Take into account as many signals as you can – plus, of course the words spoken and the tone of voice used.

You Have a Choice

Whether in a work or personal situation, if you want to get on well you have to communicate well. You cannot control the behaviour of other people. Those who act in a negative way or cause conflict may be negative people or they may be going through a temporarily difficult situation. You cannot control the way they act but

YOU CAN ALWAYS CHOOSE YOUR OWN BEHAVIOUR.

It may be very tempting to follow the other person's behaviour pattern and communicate in the way that he (or she) does – both verbally and non-verbally – but this will achieve little. In fact, it will probably make matters far worse. You can instead choose to remain your own person. If you react aggressively to the other person's aggression, there is bound to be trouble. However, if you remain in control and respond in a calm and assertive way, you will usually reduce the other person's level of anger and this, in turn, will lead to a solution to the problem.

CHAPTER SIX

Empowerment

Empowerment is simply the means by which you motivate yourself or others to perform to the very best of your (or their) ability. Considering the fact that it costs nothing – apart, of course, from your time and effort – it is one of the most effective ways of increasing productivity and encouraging innovative ideas.

Whether a company is large or small, those who work within it form one of the greatest of its potential assets. Properly encouraged, each member of a team can be guided towards making an invaluable contribution – and when the entire workforce is doing this, the company itself is bound to flourish.

Conflict between individual members of a team or between two or more teams is far less likely when each person feels motivated to do her (or his) best. So, although your time and effort will be called upon at the outset, you are likely to save yourself a great deal of time and excess stress in the long run.

As a manager, supervisor, team leader or trainer, one of the greatest skills you can acquire is that of being able to empower other people.

The person who feels motivated is going to perform far better than the one who feels apathetic.

If you become a successful motivator, not only will the company benefit by increased productivity but your own reputation is likely to be greatly enhanced. On the other hand, should your particular team fail to do well, it will be your effectiveness as a manager that will be questioned.

Before considering how best to empower other people, perhaps it is worth taking time to think about how we motivate ourselves. There are three main ways, and all of them may be adapted to working with other people. The results of each method are likely, as you will see, to vary considerably.

1. Fear

There are some individuals who rely greatly on fear as a motivator – and indeed some organizations actively encourage this. But it is a method of empowerment which can work either for or against you. Even when it appears to work in your favour, it is rarely effective in the long term.

Consider this scenario: you are a fairly good but unexceptional swimmer. You rarely swim more than four or five lengths of the local pool. One day a friend bets you £100 that you can't swim a mile. What is your reaction? Bearing in mind your previous swimming achievements, you are likely to be somewhat doubtful about your ability to keep going for a whole mile. Unsurprisingly you refuse to take the bet.

But suppose you find yourself in a boat which is sinking about a mile from the nearest shore. Your only chance of survival is to swim to land – so what do you do? With the fear of drowning as your motivator, you will probably make the attempt – and the likelihood is that you will succeed.

In that case fear would work as a motivating tool. It is unwise, however, to permit it to force you voluntarily into uncomfortable positions. In the same way, it would be unwise in the extreme to rely upon it as a means of empowering other people. Threatening someone with putting her at the top of the list when it comes to possible future redundancies may 'persuade' her to get on quickly with the particular job in hand, but it is unlikely to win her loyalty to you or the company and will therefore not be an effective long-term tool.

2. Incentive

Attempting to empower either yourself or others by means of incentive motivation is another temporarily effective measure. Incentives, of course, can be positive or negative. Just as a child may be offered a chocolate bar for doing something well or may not be allowed to watch television if she behaves badly, a workforce can be bribed with promises of extra pay or promotion for a task completed successfully. Even if they respond well to such incentives, once the job is done and the reward received, what do they have left to aim for? Very little – and so they are quite likely to slip back again into old habits.

Incentive motivation is also extremely time-consuming. When using it to empower yourself, you need to take ample time to make up your mind just what the greatest reward would be as far as you are concerned. Is it a case of more money, of fame, of promotion? If you find out what it is that would provide the spur for you, you will probably succeed in your endeavour.

When attempting to empower other people, however, you cannot assume that there is to be a single 'blanket motivating incentive' for all. Taking the trouble to discover the most appropriate reward for each person can be extremely time-consuming – particularly if your team consists of several people all with different aims in life.

3. Attitude

Attitude motivation is definitely the most consistently successful way to empower both yourself and other people. What it does is to encourage each person to *want* to perform to the best of her (or his) ability.

If you are trying to empower other people, there are three important points to keep in the forefront of your mind:

a. 'Hands-on' Experience

If someone is anxious to prove what she can do, she can become very dispirited if she is never allowed to do so. She will feel that she is not trusted and may well give up altogether. The only way she can prove that she is capable of performing a particular task is by being allowed to do it. It is up to you in such a case to stand back and let her get on with it. Of course there could be a certain risk element in doing this – but hopefully you know your staff well enough to realize the level of their competence. In any event, it is sometimes necessary to take chances in life. If this method works well, there are advantages for everyone:

- The employee will become more confident and the fact that someone – you – has shown faith in her/him will make her more eager than before to prove to you what she can do. Her skills will therefore increase and you will gain both loyalty and respect from her. Her example may also encourage other members of the team to come forward and show what they can do.

b. Showing Enthusiasm

People often have a strange idea of what motivates others. Whether we are talking about parent and child, coach to sports team or supervisor to business team, the techniques should be the same. And they should always be as positive as possible. Although we do not want to put others under too great a strain, saying something like 'Do your best' is not sufficient. Show the person you are attempting to empower that you are eager and enthusiastic about the task she is soon to undertake and about her ability to complete it successfully.

Remember the old adage, used by Dale Carnegie on his Human Relations course: 'Act enthusiastic and you'll be enthusiastic!'

c. Avoiding the 'Put-down'

When Margaret was a child, she worked hard at school. She wanted to do well for herself but, even more, she wanted to please her parents – particularly her somewhat authoritative father. And her hard work and ability to concentrate paid off – she was always in the top three or four of the class and was expected by all who taught her to go on to university.

Margaret's father, who genuinely cared for his daughter and was actually proud of her achievements, none the less had a strange idea of what would motivate her. When she came home from school, delighted at having achieved a very high grade and second place in a particular set of examinations, instead of praising her for her hard work and her ability, her father told her that he 'hoped she would do even better next time'. Is it any wonder that Margaret's confidence took a dive when even such excellent results did not satisfy her demanding parent?

All this may have taken place when Margaret was a child, but the situation is no different between adults. If you want to get the best out of someone – for individual and corporate reasons – there are specific ways of going about it. Remember that self-confidence is a fragile flower which, once damaged, is not easily repaired.

In some ways both motivating elements and demotivating elements are very similar. Each of them is catching and each of them increases – nothing remains the same.

They are catching in that the person who is feeling either positive or negative is unable to avoid demonstrating these feelings – possibly in very subtle ways which are instinctively recognized by other people, although the person may not realize he or she is revealing them.

They increase in the sense that positivity encourages further positivity and negativity encourages further negativity. Someone who is feeling confident is likely to do a good job – and this will serve to increase her confidence still further. Someone who has doubts about her ability to complete a particular task, however, is likely to approach it in such a negative way that she does not, in fact, do as well as she might. She will of course realize this and her already shaky confidence will be further shaken until one day it is completely shattered.

Let's look at some of the most common demotivating elements so that you are confident that you can recognize them and see what you can do to overcome them. Most will be within your control – although there are some that will not. All, however, will be within your understanding.

Lack of Appreciation

Perhaps this should read 'lack of *obvious* appreciation'. A supervisor, teacher or parent may be thinking that her (or his) employee, pupil or child is doing very well – but few of us are mind-readers and, unless such thoughts are made clear to the employee, pupil or child, she (or he) will presume they do not exist.

We all need obvious appreciation from the time of childhood throughout our lives, and yet so many of those to whom we look for such a reaction are either critical or else they say nothing at all. To many people, quiet praise can be far more valuable than extra money – welcome as this may be.

Edward had worked for Wilberforce & Co. for some considerable time, having progressed steadily up the company ladder as a result of his own skill and diligence.

In common with many other organizations, Wilberforce & Co. had been compelled to cut back on staff due to the problems caused by the economic climate. There had, therefore, been some redundancies.

Edward was not the most confident of men and he feared that he might be next on the list of redundancies to be made. After all, no one had ever told him that he was thought of particularly well, nor had he ever been thanked for all his extra efforts.

Having a wife and family, Edward could not bear to think of himself being without a job and so he began to look around for another while still maintaining his position with Wilberforce. Eventually he found a good position with a rival organization and handed in his notice.

The management team at Wilberforce & Co. could not understand why one of their best workers had chosen to leave. They certainly did not realize that a few appropriate words of appreciation now and then could have prevented it happening.

Poor Working Conditions

If the place in which they have to work is cramped or dull, staff automatically relate it to a lack of appreciation on the part of management. Their resulting train of thought might well be 'why should we bother when no one is bothered about us?'

A 'Big Brother' Atmosphere

Most people will accept that some sort of supervision is appropriate – particularly when a new task is being undertaken. However, should that supervision become too strict or be too obvious, it may be equated with the feeling that they are not trusted to get on with the job they are supposed to be doing. This can be quite insulting and can certainly destroy morale within a group. Once training or instruction has been given, staff need to be left alone to get on with the job they are supposed to be doing.

In such cases, of course, it is essential that the training is efficient and adequate – and also that each person there knows whom to ask should a query arise.

Low Rate of Pay

People are not stupid and it is rarely difficult for one person to discover what others are earning. If someone is earning less than others and the reasons for this are not immediately obvious, she (or he) will take this as a sign that she is considered to be worth less. All motivation will leave, along with any loyalty this employee might have felt to the company.

Problems with Regard to Status

Some organizations set great store by establishing a strict hierarchy within the company. Titles and positions seem to mean a great deal to such companies and the people working within them. I even know of one large organization where status is denoted by the number of drawers in your desk – a three-drawer person is more important than a two-drawer person, the latter being more important than a mere one-drawer person. In that same organization a one-drawer person is not allowed to address a three-drawer person but has to use a two-drawer person as an intermediary!

Although a certain amount of designation of status is inevitable, when it reaches such petty levels it can be totally demoralizing to those who feel that they are at the lower end of the scale – often with little chance of progressing upwards. They feel unappreciated and left out and are unlikely to be in the mood to do their best for the company.

Being Affected by Other Members of the Team

There is a saying that 'misery loves company' and it is true that if one member of a team is negative – for whatever reason – this is bound to rub off on those who work with her. You might think that six positive people would have a beneficial effect on one negative individual, but this is no more the case than it is that six good apples will turn a bad one ripe again.

There might be many causes of this negativity in the one person; it is up to you to find out what it is and do what you can to relieve it before it can affect everyone who comes into contact with her.

How to Counteract Demotivating Elements and Empower Those Around You

Appreciation

Take the time and trouble to demonstrate that you appreciate what is being done. Indicate it by your attitude; make it obvious by the words you use. While high achievers deserve their praise, remember that those who may be in a lower position but who give a great deal in the way of time or effort deserve praise too.

If praise and appreciation are not forthcoming, those who have made great efforts are unlikely to do so again in the future. This would be a loss to the individual, to the team and to the company.

Everyone likes to feel wanted and needed. Just a few words of appreciation or encouragement – there is no need to go over the top – can help to create this feeling and the recipient will be even more likely to do her best for you in the future.

Remember that there are also subtle ways of expressing your appreciation:

- Instead of your name alone being at the head of every document which comes from your department, acknowledge any other writers or researchers who may have contributed to it.
- If you, as head of that department, are praised for your team's efforts, make sure that you pass this praise on to all who have contributed to the actual work.
- Give fair credit to anyone who comes up with an innovative suggestion. If you fail to do so, she (or he) will probably not bother to do so in the future.

Pride in the Job

Each person should be encouraged to feel pride not only in her own part of the job being done, but in the job as a whole. As far as possible, allow everyone to share in all discussions and training so that all staff members are aware that their role is a relevant part of the greater whole.

It has been shown that people who are involved in as many different aspects of a job as possible are more empowered than those who complete a single task over and over again. The latter type of employee may become the greatest expert in the world at her particular task, but all interest in the work will soon leave her.

This has been proved predominantly in the car manufacturing industry, where it has been found that productivity increases when a team of employees works together to build an entire vehicle from scratch. This contrasts sharply with the old method where each employee performed a small range of tasks repetitively over a prolonged period.

Showing Care and Concern

When your place of work is extremely busy, it is easy to forget that employees are individual human beings too. They have personal lives which may be happy or sad, and it is a poor manager who ignores this and thinks of them simply as contributors to the output of the company. They are not simply cogs in some giant commercial wheel; they are men and women with feelings and with family responsibilities. They will appreciate it if you are able to demonstrate that you appreciate this fact.

We all have to face ups and downs in our personal lives from time to time – perhaps emotional problems, perhaps financial difficulties, perhaps lapses in health. If you are observant, it will soon become obvious if one of the members of your team is thus affected – the first indications are usually consistently bad time-keeping or obvious signs of lethargy. At such times, if you are able to show that you care about this person as an individual, she will truly appreciate it – even if initially she says nothing. If you establish good personal communication with someone who is undergoing a personal crisis, she will probably put in even greater efforts when the situation has improved in the future.

You will have to strike a balance between being available to help and not interfering where you are not wanted. Perhaps all that is needed is to allow this person time to talk to you or, if you feel that matters are beyond your scope of expertise, to persuade her (or him) to visit a good counsellor. Should any small problems arise, always try to deal with them at the first possible opportunity before they have time to intensify.

Delegate

It is often extremely difficult to delegate important tasks – particularly when you know that you can do them well and efficiently. If you are to give your team the feeling that you trust them, however, then delegate you must. The awareness that you trust them sufficiently to give them added responsibility will eventually build up their confidence.

Empowering the Group

You will be doing something very special when you boost the confidence of each individual and motivate each to do her best in return. However, it is also imperative to ensure that all these individuals are pulling in the same direction, or all your efforts will have been to no avail.

If you are to lead your team effectively it is essential that you are always seen to be their 'champion'. If you want loyalty from your team, you must be seen to be loyal to it. After all, any group of people which is not actively *for* the company can so easily turn out to be against it.

When briefing the people around you, try to brief the entire team at the same time – unless, of course, sheer numbers makes this impossible. In this way each person becomes more aware of how her role is vital to the completion of the entire task. It also ensures that there is a time for everyone to give feedback or to ask questions if there are points which could do with clarification. It is also at such team briefings that new and potentially successful ideas often emerge.

Another advantage of briefing everyone together is that, should someone become ill or unable to work, there is more likely to be someone willing and able to step into her shoes. There will no longer be a feeling of 'my job', 'your job'; the entire project will be seen as 'our job'.

Dealing with Change

Many human beings do not really like change. There are many who would prefer to stay in a situation which is less than happy than make the effort to change themselves and the way they handle things. Part of your job is to be able to spot such people and deal with them so that they do not hinder the work as a whole.

Once you have identified those who dislike change, see if you can find out what it is that bothers them. After all, if you are to empower them to do more or to do things differently, you do not want to find them hindering you at every stage.

There are a few basic reasons why such people might fear change. These are:

- They may have a general fear of anything new – whether it is a new project or a new way of doing an old job. Such fears usually arise from a sense of inferiority, often created by an earlier association with someone who has mocked or belittled them.
- If employees' confidence in themselves is low, they might believe that they would not be able to cope with learning

anything new and, rather than show themselves up, prefer to be seen as wanting to stick to the old ways.

- They may feel that they are being compelled to change against their will and that they have not been involved in the project as a whole.
- They may genuinely believe that the change proposed is the wrong one and will therefore try and prevent the change happening at all.

HOW TO DEAL WITH THOSE WHO RESIST CHANGE

- Give everyone lots of time to get used to an idea. As long as possible before the changes are to take place, send out written information giving as many details as possible and indicating the pros and cons of the change. Let others know that their opinions will be sought – and listened to.
- Call a meeting of everyone involved at which this paper can be discussed. Allow plenty of time for opinions and make it obvious that you are listening to them.
- However wrong or foolish you may consider their fears, never let them see this or you will cause immediate resentment. It is far better to be aware of any negative feelings at this stage so that you can deal with them calmly and sensibly; you do not want to destroy others' confidence by making them feel they cannot speak freely in case they are belittled.
- Taking the above into account, persuade them to be as precise as possible about any fears they may have. The more detail you demand, the more clearly they will have to think about their negative attitude.
- Deal openly with every point raised. Since there is no change that does not have disadvantages, agree with those which may be valid. You can then go on to explain the advantages and how these outweigh the negative aspects.
- After the changes have been put into effect, keep in contact with the objectors until you are sure that they have come to accept the new status quo.

Brainstorming

A brainstorming session is a good way of motivating any team. In fact, it encourages team members to motivate themselves and each other – which is even better.

Over the last few years the word 'brainstorming' has come to be taken lightly to mean any 'thinking session', whereas it is actually a specific way of going about encouraging the creation of new ideas.

Before setting out how a brainstorming session should be run, I would like you to practise thinking creatively. This is something which our education system, with its emphasis on logic and common sense, often causes us to lose the ability to do. So, stop reading now and find yourself a pen and a large sheet of paper.

Have you got them? Good. Now, allowing yourself no more than five minutes, I would like you to write down as many uses as you can think of for a plastic knitting needle – no matter how silly they may seem. Never mind if this sounds like a ridiculous waste of time; please do it.

How did you do? How many uses were you able to find for a plastic knitting needle? Is your sheet of paper full or did you stop after 'knitting'?

The current record for this exercise is 125 uses – as detailed by a delegate on one of my seminars. And he only came to a stop because the allotted time was up.

The whole point of the exercise is that no one said you had to come up with *normal* uses for a plastic knitting needle – or even that the uses had to be sensible ones. Just a few of the many with which I have been presented at seminars are:

- supporting a pot plant
- as a skewer for a kebab
- to secure a woman's long hair
- to clear a drain
- as a splint for the leg of an injured dog or cat

• for dipping in ink and using as a pen

...and so on...

Now, back to our brainstorming session.

A brainstorming group should consist of somewhere between ten and fifteen people. If there are fewer, not enough will be put forward in the way of new ideas. If there are more, the group will be too hard to control.

You will need three 'officials' – a leader to take control of the session, a time-keeper, and a recorder who will write the ideas put forward on a flip chart or white board.

Some time before the session, make sure that each participant is fully aware of the topic to be discussed – what the problem is, together with any relevant background facts.

Once the group has assembled and before starting to work on the real problem, give everyone a silly exercise (like the one about the plastic knitting needle). This will help to break the ice and prepare them to be lighthearted and creative.

Next the leader should remind everyone of the real problem to be discussed and ask all members of the group to suggest any solutions which come to them. These should be called out and written on the flip chart by the recorder. It is very important to emphasize that the solutions do *not* have to be sensible – or even feasible – just the first thing that the problem brings to mind. About 20 minutes should be allowed for this stage (the time-keeper should make sure that time limits are strictly adhered to).

The whole point of a brainstorming session is that people should be allowed to say absolutely anything without someone else criticizing them or their ideas or reminding them that their proposals would be unworkable. Indeed, the leader should quash any critical comments which might arise and should encourage participants to allow their imaginations to run freely so that anything can be said.

(A sensible solution is often to be found buried in what may at first seem like a ridiculous suggestion. One of the larger building societies was running a brainstorming session on how to encourage more people to use their branches during the week at non-peak times – that is, not at lunchtime or immediately after work. As it was felt that this time could well be used by mothers of young children, one of the ideas brainstormed was that the branch should instal a giant playpen just inside the entrance so that mothers could deposit their child there on the way in and pick them up again on the way out – thus being able to conduct their transactions unencumbered.

From this somewhat farfetched idea came the concept of having play tables complete with building blocks and other toys for the children to sit at while their mothers conducted their business – a sensible solution born of a seemingly unworkable idea.)

After a break, the group should reassemble and each idea written on the flip chart should be discussed sensibly – being broken down into concept and practicality. Time should be spent on even the most outrageous suggestions to see whether there might be the germ of a good idea buried within them.

Brainstorming is effective as a form of empowerment for many reasons:

- During the session everyone is equal and has as much right to express her (or his) ideas as anyone else.
- Each member of the team will be aware that she is going to have her ideas put forward and discussed.
- Because of the lighthearted atmosphere at such sessions, a feeling of bonhomie and combined purpose is often generated among members of a team – even those who do not know each other well.
- There is the excitement of knowing that it is possible for such sessions to produce excellent and innovative ideas. This excitement is often carried through into the normal working days which follow, thus encouraging people to be more creative and enthusiastic than usual.
- Individual growth is encouraged which can have a long-lasting beneficial effect on individuals as well as the company.
- People can be encouraged to look at topics as challenges rather than as problems to be overcome.

- There are less likely to be conflicts between people who have worked together in a brainstorming session, so this is a way of managing conflict in a positive and interesting fashion.

CHAPTER SEVEN

Conflict-causing Personalities

Everyone can have a bad day or a time when his (or her) behaviour leads to conflict – whether major or minor. But there are certain types of people who are more likely than others to be responsible for conflict within a group or team.

For the sake of this chapter it has naturally been necessary to describe these people in fairly black-and-white terms. Naturally not everyone conforms *precisely* to one of these descriptions. Indeed, many people exhibit characteristics of two or more. None the less, the descriptions given here, together with the best ways of dealing with them, should help you when you are confronted by a conflict situation within the group or team you are managing.

The Aggressor

This is someone who is a verbal bully and who is likely to shout, swear, thump the table or point the finger in order to emphasize a point – *his* point. He causes unhappiness and friction within the team in general and may become involved in a one-to-one confrontation with another member of the team. The effects of such a confrontation – whoever comes out the 'winner' – may well last for a long time, certainly far beyond the period of the dispute itself.

This type of person usually has a good brain and is a hard worker. He is often right in his decisions – and always thinks he is. He tends to make snap decisions and then refuses to deviate from them, seeing such deviation as a sign of weakness in himself. This is something he refuses to tolerate.

He causes conflict because of his behaviour. When he is aggressive, the people with whom he works may well shout back at him, refuse to work with him or simply avoid him altogether.

HOW TO DEAL WITH AN AGGRESSOR

- The first thing to remember is that, unless you happen to be a naturally aggressive person yourself (and I do hope you're not), just shouting back won't achieve a thing. You will be up against a real champion and therefore unlikely to win any shouting match and, at the end of it all, he will have an extremely low opinion of you and your capabilities.

- Be assertive when dealing with an Aggressor. Use such phrases as 'In my opinion', which help him to believe that, while you do not necessarily agree with him, you are conceding that he might have a point. If you are able to remain calm yet determined in your manner – no matter what he says or how he acts – he is more likely to respect you.

- If, because of his nature, he interrupts you while you are speaking, stop and point out to him that he has done so before continuing. But avoid doing this in a confrontational manner. Something like 'George, you're interrupting me...' before continuing with what you were saying is usually sufficient.

- Be aware of your body language. When dealing with an aggressive individual it is psychologically important to maintain direct level eye contact with him. So, if he comes to see you, ask him to sit down (if you are seated). If he won't do so, then you must stand in order to keep this eye level constant.

The Passive Aggressor

This person is quite different in that he is not outwardly aggressive in the sense that he does not shout, bang tables, but the
motivation (since aggression is all about power and control)
behind his actions and behaviour is just the same.

A passive aggressor manages to block progress at every turn.
He never volunteers to do anything; he never puts forward any
ideas or suggestions of his own; he never works as hard as he is
capable of doing.

If you try to draw this person out and make him feel that he
is an essential part of the whole team, you will get very little
response. Ask him how things are going and he will probably
answer 'All right' – which tells you nothing. He is not the person to volunteer information at any time.

HOW TO DEAL WITH A PASSIVE AGGRESSOR

- It is essential to speak to him alone, lest his lack of communication so infuriates others that they decide to speak for him.
- Put him on the spot with your questions; ask those to which
  there can be no monosyllabic or non-committal answer.
- Ask him if he has any ideas or suggestions with regard to the
  work currently in progress – and then keep quiet so that he is
  eventually compelled to answer. It is a common trick of a passive aggressor to say nothing until the person speaking to him
  feels that he (or she) must speak in order to break the silence.
  Keep your body language open and friendly but remain silent
  until he replies.

The Chronic Absentee

The reasons behind the repeated absence from work of a single
individual may be many and varied. They may also be fabricated
or genuine. Even when the reasons have been fabricated, however, there is usually a genuine problem hidden behind them –
perhaps one that the absentee does not feel able or prepared to
discuss with you.

In other cases, of course, there are those who know that they are entitled to a statutory amount of sick leave and, even if they haven't had a single day of illness, feel that they have the right to the extra time off – as though it were an additional holiday allowance.

The genuine problems for repeated absences include:

- problems at work – perhaps the person feels unable to cope or that he does not fit in with other members of the team; or perhaps he finds his part of the work repetitive and boring
- problems at home – his concerns might be for the health and welfare of one or more members of his family; he might have financial difficulties or be going through a divorce or separation;
- problems of stress – which could be caused by either of the above or by the level of pressure he is under at that specific time. Stress manifests itself in many different ways, including affecting the mental, physical or emotional health of the sufferer.

HOW TO DEAL WITH A CHRONIC ABSENTEE

- The first and most important thing to do is to recognize the problem and try to identify the cause. An initial step – even before confronting the absentee – is to observe whether the absences take place on a regular day or when a regular task is due to be performed. This may well give you a much-needed clue.
- The next stage is to tackle the absentee himself in an assertive but never accusatory or aggressive way. Let him know that you are aware of the number of absences (showing documented proof, if necessary) and then ask whether there is a problem about which he might like to talk.
- What comes next will depend upon the response you get from the absentee. If he is forthcoming and tells you that there *is* a problem, you may find yourself having to make a choice. If the problem is work-related, you will be able to deal with that yourself. If it concerns his home and family life – and if he is

willing to talk about it – you may feel able to handle that as well. On the other hand, particularly if you have had little or no specific training in counselling techniques, you might prefer to refer him to an independent counsellor.

More and more companies these days are employing the services of a qualified counsellor when members of staff appear to be under severe stress or to have obvious emotional problems with which they need help. Even if the supervisor or personnel officer has had some training in this field, it has been found that few employees are willing to confide in these people. With redundancy still rife and fear of it ever present in most people, they see personnel officers, welfare officers and supervisors as part of 'the organization' and feel that, if they tell them too much about their problems, they will be seen at some future time as a 'weak link' in the corporate chain and may find themselves top of the next redundancy list.

If it appears that the absences are arising because of problems to do with work, obviously you will do what you can to solve them. At the same time, however, it is as well to point out to the employee in question that, even if he appears to be working on his own, he is, in fact, involved in the work of the company and his repeated absences are letting other people down.

If you have reason to believe that the absences are not caused by genuine reasons at all but arise because that particular person is lazy or feels he has the right to use all his statutory sick leave, be a little devious before confronting him. After all, you might be wrong.

On one of the days when he does not turn up for work, try telephoning his home some time in the middle of the day. If no one answers, you might have reason to believe that your suspicions have some validity. If the employee does answer, however, all you need to say is that you were telephoning to see how he was.

The Person Who Makes Too Many Errors

We are all capable of making mistakes, either through carelessness or lack of knowledge. But there are some people who seem to spend their lives leaping from one disastrous error to another. Even if these mistakes are immediately obvious and something is done about them right away, they can take time and cost money. If they are covered up, however, in such a way that they do not come to light until some future date, the costs can be far greater – both financially (as any work which followed the commission of the error might have to be re-done) and also in terms of the morale of the people involved.

There may be many reasons why one individual repeatedly commits errors and, particularly if you think he has the potential to be a useful member of the team, it is worth taking the time to discover these reasons. They could include:

- nervousness: In the same way that some students who have revised thoroughly for an examination go to pieces and are unable to think clearly when they actually come face to face with the exam, there are those employees who understand fully well what they are supposed to do but who are so nervous of making a mistake that they almost make it happen.
- failure to understand training: There can be many reasons for this. Some people are naturally slow learners – although in many cases once a piece of knowledge has been absorbed it is well remembered. Perhaps the training itself was not as efficient as it might have been – this is something you can check up on. Perhaps the person giving the training did not allow sufficient time or opportunity for feedback or the asking of questions. If this sort of feedback is not specifically requested, some people are too nervous to volunteer it, feeling possibly that they would be showing themselves up as unintelligent.
- having too much to do: You will often find that new or the most junior members of staff – particularly if they are extremely willing and anxious to be helpful – take on far more than they can cope with and, in an effort to complete it all and please everybody, make innumerable mistakes.

- being easily distracted: While some people are quite capable of maintaining their own little oasis of calm in a busy workplace, others find they are easily distracted by anything and everything – from the ringing of someone else's telephone to a conversation between two other people. Naturally, the more frequently such a person's concentration is broken the more likely it is that he will make mistakes when he again turns his attention to the work in hand.

HOW TO DEAL WITH SOMEONE WHO MAKES TOO MANY MISTAKES

- You should be able to recognize the difference between someone who is just slipshod and careless about his work and someone who is trying hard and yet still seems to make mistake after mistake. In the case of the latter, take the time to approach him and ask whether he has any particular problems – in or out of work. If you feel that this is someone worth encouraging, remember the psychological formula of positive-negative-positive when speaking to him and implying any form of criticism. In other words, you should always start and end on an encouraging note, even if you have to be critical in between. In this way you will not damage the possibly fragile self-esteem of the person you are talking to.

  A possible example might be:

  Joanna, I'm delighted to see how much of our process you have been able to pick up since you arrived here. And we all really appreciate your willingness to help whenever you can. However, I do feel that too many mistakes appear to be creeping into your own work. Why don't we have a chat about it? I'm sure we can sort things out between us so that you can develop the potential I know you have and become a really valuable member of the team.

- Look into the need for further training. If you are convinced that any training which has already been given is perfectly adequate and allows time for questions and feedback, perhaps some extra help on a one-to-one basis would be beneficial.

- Consider the personality of the person who is making all these mistakes. Is he particularly nervous – and, if so, does this nervousness seem to apply across the board or does your observation tell you that he is especially in awe of one specific person? If the nervousness is general, it might be worth sending him for assertiveness training. If it seems to be heightened by contact with one particular person, it would be beneficial to explore the possibility of some sort of conflict between the two of them.

- If he is obviously trying to do too much, check that he is not being given work by several different people – work which he does not admit that he cannot cope with. Tell him that you will do what you can to ensure that he is not asked to do more than is possible – and keep your promise.

- Appeal to his sense of co-operation with the rest of the team as well as his pride in his own work, and ask him to ensure that he checks thoroughly what he does and asks about anything he does not fully understand.

Negative People

Although everyone has bouts of negativity from time to time, there are two principal types of consistently negative persons to deal with here.

1) The individual who is aggressively negative. He is always critical of other people and their achievements, using phrases such as, 'You're doing that all wrong' or 'That's a stupid idea!' While being eager to point out the negative, however, he never seems to have any positive ideas of his own.

   Someone who is regularly aggressively negative is a basically insecure person – as all bullies are. Anyone with a vestige of confidence in himself really has no need to show such aggression to others. These constant criticisms – while aimed at other people and making them feel bad – are really designed to make the critic himself feel better.

2) The second type of negative person is not aggressive at all but can have an extremely depressing effect on anyone with whom he comes into contact. Whatever is suggested, he foresees failure. 'That will never work,' he says. Or, 'That would be a complete waste of time.' Naturally he never comes up with any better solutions of his own.

This person may well do anything asked of him reasonably well, but he will never allow himself to be cheered up – because, when it comes to it, he doesn't really want to be. He prefers to remain in his melancholy state.

HOW TO DEAL WITH AN AGGRESSIVELY NEGATIVE PERSON

- Whatever you do, don't try to be as aggressive as he is; it just won't work. After all, he has had far more practice than you and he can probably do it better – which would put you at a disadvantage should you wish to try anything else.
- If he comes to you making aggressively critical remarks about other people or their work, let him go on until he runs out of steam and then ask him an assertive question – 'What makes you say that?' or 'Why do you feel that is the case?', for example. Because he is unlikely to have any real justification for his venom other than to boost his own ego, he is unlikely to know what to say and will probably start to bluster. The fact that he does so will tell you that his negative attitude is unfounded and unimportant and that you can safely ignore his remarks. When this has happened a few times, he is less likely to make them.

HOW TO DEAL WITH A DEPRESSIVE/NEGATIVE PERSON

- Do something about it as soon as possible. If you allow him to go on he will end up depressing the entire team and work will be slower and far less productive.
- Ask him to explain just why he thinks a particular idea will not work. This is worth doing, as there may be occasions when he is right and wasted effort could be avoided.
- Then put him on the spot and ask him to suggest an improved solution of his own. If he says he cannot think of one, insist

that he goes away to think about it and provides you with a list of alternative solutions – giving him a deadline by which time this list has to be completed and handed over.

- If he comes up with any improved or workable solutions, be sure to give him credit for having done so. Someone this negative really needs to have his self-esteem boosted.

The Chatterbox

This is often someone who is outgoing and friendly and who is liked by most people – although he may well drive them to distraction at the same time. The trouble arises because he is not aware of just how irritating his behaviour is – and often people do not want to hurt his feelings, so no one actually tells him. None the less, because he is so annoying he can unwittingly cause conflict.

The chatterbox will breeze into the workplace, full of gossip or inconsequential news and, without stopping to take account of whether other people are engrossed in their work or not, will approach one or more of them and start to impart this news. Obviously this can be highly distracting, disrupting trains of thought at significant moments.

No one really wants to hurt this basically pleasant person, so in many cases people say nothing until they cannot bear it any longer, at which point they may be quite aggressive, releasing all the tension which has been building up and causing the chatterbox more distress than would previously have been the case.

HOW TO DEAL WITH A CHATTERBOX

- Don't tackle him in front of everyone, but make an arrangement to see him later in the day. There are two reasons for this: first, there is no need to humiliate or upset him in front of everyone else and, secondly, the mysterious reason for this meeting will arouse his interest to such a degree that, when you do meet, he is more likely to remain silent in order to hear what you have to say.

- When you do meet, begin by emphasizing that you have only his interests at heart and that you hope what you have to say will not upset him in any way. This will help to maintain his level of interest plus it will indicate to him that you are empathizing with him and are on his side.
- Remembering the positive/negative/positive formula, point out to him:

  1 that he is liked and appreciated as a pleasant and caring person,
  2 that people find his way of interrupting their trains of thought disruptive and irritating,
  3 that you are sure he probably has not realized what he has been doing and the effect it has had and, now that he knows, you are sure he will make the effort to change.

The Do-nothing

This is another likable person who has the best interests of the team at heart but who is so scared of making a mistake (thereby letting the other members of the team down) that he tends to stand back and do nothing. He may often appear lazy but this is not really the case. He can prove to be quite efficient in areas where he has total confidence.

In many instances this person will, however, do nothing at all – hoping that the task or the problem will go away by itself. This it often appears to do, as others get so tired of waiting for him to do something that they give up and tackle it themselves.

It is worth taking the time and trouble to help someone like this overcome his problem as, once this has been done, he is likely to be a careful and efficient member of the team.

HOW TO DEAL WITH A DO-NOTHING
- See if you can find out what it is that is worrying him. Is it the fact that he might make a mistake, thereby letting down the person he was supposed to be helping?
- Suggest that, until he feels more sure of himself, he discusses

what he intends to do with you. This should provide him with the reassurance he requires to be able to proceed.

- At the same time, he should be encouraged to seek help in building up his self-esteem in general so that he is no longer so full of doubt.

The Unreliable Person

This is another extremely agreeable person who wants only to like and be liked by others. Because of this desire, he not only agrees to do whatever anyone asks of him but goes out of his way to volunteer to undertake further tasks and to offer to help any or all of his colleagues. When he makes these arrangements, he genuinely means to carry them all out but, having taken on far too much, he is naturally unable to do so.

This causes people to lose patience with him and to get annoyed. Because this is something he hates, he promises even more in order to please them – and thus the vicious circle goes round again.

Irritating as he may be, this is another person with whom it is worth taking time and trouble. His very willingness to help can be turned to great advantage once he learns to recognize his own capabilities and limitations, and comes to see that he is actually alienating the people whose friendship he seeks by repeatedly letting them down.

Another trait of this type of person is to make self-deprecating jokes behind which he hides. Paying attention to these jokes can often provide you with clues as to his true feelings.

HOW TO DEAL WITH AN UNRELIABLE PERSON
- Let him know that he is liked as an individual and that he does not have to 'buy' people's approval by undertaking every suggested task.
- Suggest that he spends more time thinking about how long each task is likely to take him and creating a realistic personal time-table so that he does not take on more than he can actually complete. Remind him that people would rather be told

at the outset that he did not have the time to do something than to discover it as a deadline approaches.

- Look behind his jokes to discover his true feelings about himself and, if you feel he needs help with regard to his confidence, try to arrange for this.

The Time-Waster

There are various types of time-wasters. Some people have good intentions but find themselves easily distracted. Some misunderstand what is wanted of them in the first place. But the one we are dealing with here is the deliberate time-waster who thinks nothing of using the company's time to make a personal telephone call, fill in his football pools coupon or finish his crossword.

In addition, although he would not dream of taking money or goods which do not belong to him, this type of time-waster will 'steal' minutes here and there – although he probably does not realize what he is doing. The 15-minute coffee break will take 20 minutes; the hour for lunch drags on for 70 minutes; he might arrive five minutes late in the morning or leave five minutes early in the evening. He does not see this as doing anything wrong, arguing that 'Everyone does it, don't they?' He does not realize how many hours these stolen minutes can add up to over the course of a week, a month or a year.

HOW TO DEAL WITH A TIME-WASTER

- Remind him that in business time equals money. Showing him on paper the number of hours lost in a year if he merely extends each coffee and lunch break by five minutes may bring him to his senses.
- Point out how unfair he is being to everyone else on the team by wasting time. In addition to delaying progress on the current project, he may be causing them to miss out on bonuses if they fail to complete work on time.
- Use the 'carrot and stick' approach. Remind him that, as he already achieves a certain amount, he would achieve so much

more if he were to work the required number of hours each and every day. Remind him, too, that those who do not complete their work on time might find themselves missing out on promotion or bonus payments in the future.

The Resentful Person

We have all met people with a chip on their shoulder who think that everyone is getting a far better deal than they are – and that it is not fair.

Some people resent authority figures in general, but it is just possible that, in this case, there could be personal resentment of you in particular. (Try not to assume that the latter is the case. Of course it is possible, but you are far more likely to find that you are dealing with a more general resentment).

Personal resentment sometimes arises when one member of a group is promoted to supervisor; someone else in that group might find it hard to take direction from a former equal.

There can be many other reasons for resentment:

- bigotry: The individual may have been raised with the belief that prejudice against a particular race or culture is acceptable. No one can control a person's inner feelings, but open evidence of such bigotry must not be permitted in the workplace.
- prejudice against women (or, I suppose, these days, against men – but it is more usually the former): Some men still find it extremely difficult to take direction from a woman – or even to work alongside her as an equal.
- prejudice against younger people: To some, it may appear to be a sign of failure on their own part if younger people are either on equal footing with or in a superior position to them.

HOW TO DEAL WITH A RESENTFUL PERSON
- Arrange a private discussion where you can ask him to explain his attitude. Find out whether his ill-feeling is towards you in particular and, if so, why. If, for example, he finds it difficult

to accept that you, as a former peer, are now in a superior position to him, he may feel that any praise you give him is patronizing while failure to acknowledge what he does is a personal slight. Point out to him that he is putting you in an impossible situation.

- If his resentment is a result of prejudice towards a particular race, creed, culture, gender or age group, you need to leave him in no doubt that overt indications of such prejudice will not be tolerated and that, however good his work, he will be putting his own position in jeopardy should he continue to display them.

You may feel that dealing with such potential conflict-causing people is going to take a great deal of time and effort on your part. Perhaps it will at the outset. But it will be time well spent because, if you play your part efficiently and well, you will be creating a team who will pull together and be relatively conflict-free. This will not only be of tremendous benefit to the company but will reflect well on the entire department as well as upon you as an individual.

CHAPTER EIGHT

Supervising

Whatever your official title – manager, supervisor, group leader, etc. – being in charge of other people is a very important job. It will be your task to create a team with members who are capable of working together towards a single goal.

Some companies like to promote people to supervisory level from within the organization – even from within an existing group. Others prefer to bring in a completely new face from outside. There are advantages and disadvantages to be found in each way of doing things.

Promotion from Within

ADVANTAGES:

- The new supervisor is already familiar with the company and its policies.
- She (or he) also knows quite a bit about the people she will be supervising – their personalities and their capabilities.
- She will have the confidence which comes with knowing that she has been selected by people who have known her for some time and who, by their choice, have shown that they have faith in her ability to perform the job well.
- She already has experience of the company itself – the way it is run, its ethos and its policies.

DISADVANTAGES:

- It may be difficult for those who have previously worked alongside the new supervisor to accept that she (or he) is now in a position to tell them what to do.
- There may be some resentment among former peers, particularly if one or more of them had hoped to be given the supervisory role themselves.
- The new supervisor might find it difficult to give direction to anyone who had formerly been on equal footing with her, especially if that person has been with the company longer than she herself has.

Promotion from Outside

ADVANTAGES:

- Because she (or he) is coming fresh to the company, the new supervisor is less likely to experience resentment from the team.
- She can be secure in the knowledge that she has been deliberately selected for the position by people who knew precisely what they were looking for.
- She is likely to bring with her fresh ideas about policies or techniques which may liven up the team and its efforts.

DISADVANTAGES:

- It will take a little time for her to settle into the company, to become aware of the way things are done.
- She will have no knowledge of the team she is to be supervising – personalities, background, special skills, etc.
- Some members of the team might be antagonistic towards an outsider, especially if she is younger than they are.

The Role of Supervisor

However you have been appointed – from within or from outside – it is essential that you understand the scope of your role from the very outset. As each organization expects different degrees of responsibility and accountability from its supervisory staff, it is up to you to seek clarification from those who appointed you in the first place. Ideally, what is expected of you should be set out in writing so that there can be no confusion at a later date when those above you may have moved on and themselves been replaced.

If you feel that there is any part of your duty which you are not yet fit to perform, it is up to those who appointed you to ensure that you receive appropriate training to ensure that you are adequately prepared to fulfil your role in the best way possible.

It is also essential that you know from the outset when you are supposed to deal with problems yourself and when you are supposed to report upwards.

A successful supervisor must have many skills:

GOOD COMMUNICATION

- Regular discussions are a vital part of the supervisory role. You need to talk frequently to the members of your team – both as a group and individually. This will help them to feel that they are working *with* you as opposed to *for* you – which they might resent.
- Listen to the ideas of team members. If you think they are good, say so and pass them on for further consideration. If they are capable of being improved, discuss this with the team. If not, don't pass them on.
- Make regular reports to management about the team's progress – but never pass on any personal confidences or you will lose their trust for ever.
- Ensure that each member of the team knows precisely what is expected of her (or him). This will involve explanation and feedback as there should be no 'grey areas' of doubt.

DELEGATION

- Drawing on your own knowledge and experience, make a decision as to who is best able to perform a particular task, explain what is required – and then leave her (or him) to get on with it. You may find this difficult to do as it can be hard to let go, especially if this is a job you have been doing yourself. The delegatee is likely to be slower in the beginning and may even do it less well – but she will only learn and improve if she is allowed to carry it through herself.

- Having delegated a task, let the other person know that, although you will not interfere, you will be available for consultation if needed.

- There is naturally a certain amount of risk in allowing someone else to perform a task for the first time – although it is a risk you need to take. You can, however, minimize this risk by careful planning, good choice of delegatee plus adequate explanation or training as needed.

- If a task is a complicated one, you may need to teach it in stages, allowing the other person to build up aptitude – and therefore confidence – a bit at a time.

- Training for a task you are delegating should be your responsibility. Whether this training is carried out by you personally or by a special training consultant brought in from elsewhere will depend very much on the size of the organization, the way they prefer to do things and the type of job being delegated.

- Remember that no one is indispensable and that others can learn to do those jobs you previously undertook yourself. Not only will this be good for the members of your team but it will release you to perform those tasks which are your responsibility alone.

- Planning for delegation is essential. You need to decide:

  what you want to accomplish
  what resources you have available
  how best those resources should be used.

SIX STEPS TO EFFECTIVE DELEGATION:

1) Decide which tasks can be handed over to other people.
2) Select the appropriate individual for each task, taking into account her (or his) experience and ability.
3) Give her clear explanations of what is expected of her, training her if necessary. Give her a chance to put any questions she might have.
4) Decide on a deadline for completion of the task and acceptable standards of achievement. Make sure the delegatee is aware of these.
5) Reassure her that you will answer any queries, deal with problems and be available to give guidance where needed.
6) Keep an eye on her progress but never be tempted to step in and take over. If problems arise, help her to solve them herself. This will teach her far more than taking the task away from her and doing it yourself.

TRAINING:

- Before trying to train others, make sure you yourself fully understand the topic.
- In addition to explaining *what* they need to know, explain *why* they need to know it. This will help them to make more sense of the subject and the role it plays.
- Plan well, taking time to consider which people are best suited to be trained for which tasks.
- Always allow ample time for training. Include demonstrations where possible.
- Remember that we retain best those things which we have the chance to see, hear, consider, talk about and do for ourselves.
- Break up training sessions into smaller time-chunks. It has been shown that we remember best whatever we learn at the beginning and end of a session. It makes more sense, therefore, to have a number of beginnings and ends. It has also been shown that concentration lapses seriously after about 45 minutes to one hour. Several short sessions with gaps of at least ten minutes between them are thus more effective than one or two long ones.

- If it can be arranged, try to arrange for training to take place away from the workplace itself. For one thing, there are less likely to be interruptions which will break the learning pattern and, for another, it is psychologically better to separate training from daily work in as many ways as possible.
- Be patient. Some people are naturally slower to learn new facts or techniques – but this does not mean that, once the knowledge has been acquired, they will not be able to perform new tasks excellently. Some are inclined to be nervous when they find themselves in a learning environment, and this nervousness may cause them to make mistakes which they would not otherwise make.
- If you are the one doing the training, make as much use as possible of participation, role play, visual aids, etc.
- The more you (or the trainer) can maintain a high level of enthusiasm, the more enthusiastic the trainees will be about the new skills they are learning.
- Errors are bound to occur. These can be used as highly effective learning tools. Never belittle or humiliate anyone for making mistakes.
- Try to vary your pace and technique during the course of the training. There is nothing more boring than sitting in an uncomfortable seat and listening to someone speak *at* you for long periods of time.
- Allow ample time for questions, comments and feedback. It is important to ensure that each stage of the training is understood by everyone before you progress to the next.
- A good trainer will always be aware that, no matter how experienced she (or he) may be, she can always learn from those she is training.

MOTIVATION

- Keeping your team motivated is essential as, if you fail to do so, things will slip backwards. Nothing remains constant so, without progress, there will be regression.
- The more eager and enthusiastic you can be about the work being done – and the more you are able to demonstrate this

eagerness and enthusiasm to your team members – the more likely you will be to arouse the same feelings in them.

- Let them know that all efforts and achievements are recognized. Some people have relatively minor and less spectacular tasks to perform than others, but it is just as important to let these people see that you appreciate what they are doing. Others might be a little slower or find things a little more difficult; if you know that they are doing their best and that they are improving, be sure that they are aware of this too.

- Your team should always know that you have complete faith in their ability to succeed. This will inspire greater confidence in them and this positivity will, in fact, make them more likely to succeed in whatever they are doing.

- However keen you are for a task to be completed, once training has been given let the team members get on with things for themselves. There is little more demoralizing than having someone at your shoulder and watching everything you do.

COUNSELLING/ADVISING

- This is a vital part of the supervisor's role. In fact, if you do not find that the members of your team come to you for advice it is time to wonder whether you are doing your job well.

- Unless you are a trained counsellor, there may well be problems you are unable to deal with personally. In such cases you need to have access to information which will tell you who can deal with them and to see that the person with the problem is given this information or put in contact with the relevant person.

- You may like to discuss with senior management the possibility of employing a professional counsellor on a regular basis – particularly if your company is a large one. Many organizations now do this, as it has been found that individual members of staff may be reluctant to talk to a senior employee of the same company about problems which may be troubling them.

- It is important for you to know each individual member of

your team and for each of them to feel that she (or he) knows you. Team members need to realize that you are taking an interest in them yet not prying.

- Trust is important. Anyone who comes to speak to you must be aware that you will honour all confidences. You may feel it appropriate to suggest that she (or he) speaks to another person about her problem – but it is something you do not have the right to do on her behalf (unless, of course, she specifically requests this).

- If you think your team are unaware of what is available in the way of counselling or advice, it is worth calling a meeting to point this out to them and to let them know that you are there and ready to help. (If your company – and therefore your team – is small, you might prefer to approach each member individually rather than calling a separate meeting).

- Be a good listener. Any trained counsellor knows that she (or he) is little more than a facilitator and that her role is to help individuals to help themselves.

LOYALTY

- The supervisor has to be – and be seen to be – loyal to both her (or his) team and to the company. It is the only way she will gain the respect and co-operation of both.

- If you feel that something demanded or stated by those representing the company is unfair to one or more members of your team, you must say so.

- If, on the other hand, you believe that someone in your team is not pulling her weight, you must say this too.

As you can see from the above, you will have to bring all your assertiveness training to bear if you are to keep the peace, avoid conflict between parties – and avoid being one of the causes of conflict yourself.

BEING A MEMBER OF THE TEAM

- In addition to fulfilling the supervisory duties such as giving instructions or delegating work, you must be seen to be playing your own part as a member of the team if you are not to cause resentment among the other team members.

- Maintaining your own standards is important. If you let yours slip, you will soon find that those of the other team members slip too. They will always take their lead from you in this respect – even if they are not always consciously aware that they are doing so.

- Remember that you are responsible both for your own personal results and also for those of your team.

DEALING WITH PROBLEMS

- Problems should be confronted as soon as you are aware of them if they are not to escalate.

- If the problem is between two or more people and a conflict arises, interview each of them separately before setting up a counselling interview. At a counselling interview, each individual is given time to state her grievances and how they make her feel. Because each of them addresses you, rather than each other, you can control the interview, ensuring that tempers are not raised and that interruptions are avoided. Each person is then encouraged to state what outcome or change she would like to see come about, and it is your task to encourage a spirit of compromise so that everyone leaves the interview satisfied.

- If the problems concern work – as opposed to other workers – it is up to you to listen to concerns and, if you consider them valid, to approach higher levels of management so that they understand the feelings of the staff. You may be able to set up a meeting between the two groups.

- Remember that even those problems which do not appear to concern work or the workplace will affect what is achieved. Someone who is experiencing difficulties in her personal life will soon be under great stress – and this in turn can lead to physical problems causing chronic absenteeism. Even if things do not go this far and the person manages to come into work every day, she is unlikely to feel fit enough to give of her best.

You will no doubt be aware that the role of supervisor involves many skills and that it is vital at all times to remain assertive and to communicate well with those around you. It can be one of the most trying – but also one of the most rewarding – roles in the modern workplace.

CHAPTER NINE

Appraisal

Many of us are the worst possible judges of how we are coping with situations and how we come across to other people – and this is not really surprising as we often observe things only from our own subjective viewpoint.

Some people may be working extremely hard but not realize that they are alienating colleagues because of some flaw in their attitude – often unintentional and unrecognized. Others who are deliberately not pulling their weight may think that they are getting away with achieving less than they should while, in truth, their behaviour has been noted by those around them.

To avoid the conflict which may be caused in such situations, it is up to the manager or supervisor to ensure that his (or her) team is content and functions well as a single entity by ensuring that everyone knows just where he or she stands. Hence the use in many organizations of *the appraisal system*.

An appraisal is not intended to be an attack on any individual employee. Nor is it an excuse simply to point out failings. Even though other members of a team may be asked to contribute their feelings about a particular member, by no means is a character assassination intended or desired.

Most organizations will carry out appraisals every six months – although some prefer to do it annually, while still others will use the system as a follow-up to each major project.

Not all companies are clear about what an appraisal really is. It should not be a salary discussion, even though what arises during the appraisal interview may be used at a later date during salary negotiations. Nor is the completed appraisal form intended to be a secret document passed between the manager or team leader and senior management. That is not an appraisal.

An appraisal should be a discussion between a manager and an individual employee. Its aim is to help both the company and the employee get the most out of each other. Progress so far should be reviewed and the future of the employee discussed, concentrating on such topics as promotion, changes in attitude, training needs, etc. It also presents an opportunity to discuss problems on either side and to bring to the fore difficulties involving the employee or the company which might have been recognized by other members of staff.

Every attempt should be made to maintain a non-emotional approach to the appraisal form and interview. Any criticism which may be felt to be necessary should be constructive and should be given and taken as such.

The appraisal interview itself should be an opportunity for two-way communication rather than being a chance for a member of management to talk to the employee who, for his (or her) part, just has to sit there and take it. If the employee has anything to say in return, the manager should be prepared to listen to what is said in a positive and open-minded way. Similarly, the employee should be given ample time to offer feedback – particularly in response to any criticism which might arise. Such criticism, if any, should be given in a calm and assertive way so that the employee realizes that it is intended to be helpful and part of the general learning process rather than criticism for its own sake.

By the end of the appraisal interview, both parties should be aware of the employee's progress and achievements within the company as well as of any changes he or she might be expected to make to gain higher achievements.

Stages of an Effective Appraisal Interview

1. Preparation

Proper preparation is of vital importance and there is no excuse at all for not carrying out such preparation. A good team leader will:

- read the files in order to remind himself of the history to date of the particular employee
- study any previous appraisal forms, noting any progress (or otherwise) which may have been made

2. Discussion with Fellow Employees

The employee/appraisee should be discussed with his (or her) colleagues with a view to understanding the type of relationships which exist within the team. It is important that other members of the team are reminded that they should remain assertive and give their opinions on both the positive and negative aspects of their colleague. It is also important that it is clearly understood by all concerned that this is a normal part of the process to be treated with seriousness and that each person will receive the same treatment when his turn for appraisal arises.

3. Appraisal Form – Part One

Complete Part One of your company's appraisal form. (A typical one is given below, but naturally this may need to be altered to suit the requirements of your organization). As you will see, the first part covers both the employee's personal and practical skills; this should be completed before the interview itself. The second part is completed during the interview and covers the employee's own feelings about his (or her) work and any aims and ambitions for the future. Send a copy of the appraisal form, with Part One completed, to the appraisee in advance of the interview. Not only is this a courtesy, but it gives him an opportunity to formulate any comments or questions and to think about his views on the questions in Part Two.

4. Arranging the Appraisal

Make arrangements for the appraisal interview itself. Obviously it is wise not to choose your busiest day of the week or any other awkward time, such as when the team is approaching the completion of an important project. The aim is to make the interview as relaxed as possible for both appraiser and employee, so you will not want to be watching the clock while it is in progress. For the same reason it is best not to arrange too many appraisal interviews for the same day.

5. Creating the Right Atmosphere

The atmosphere in the interview room should not be threatening to the appraisee, so make sure that the furniture is set out in a welcoming fashion. Avoid such aggressive arrangements as having your chair larger and higher than the employee's, or sitting behind a desk which is raised on a platform, as this is intimidating to the interviewee. Keep any arrangement of furniture as informal – and therefore relaxed – as possible.

Ensure that everyone knows that there are to be no interruptions during appraisal interviews.

6. Starting the Interview

Begin the interview by having a discussion based on what has been written on Part One of the appraisal form. Whatever is written there, whether favourable or otherwise, should not form the basis of an argument but of sensible discussion. If the comments have been less favourable than the employee would have wished, he (or she) may begin by being somewhat defensive and may even become belligerent – so it is extremely important that you remain calm and assertive at all times. If you can encourage the employee to do the same, so much the better. After all, the outcome desired here is a positive one for both the employee and the company – a win/win situation – so there is nothing to be gained by arguments or hurt feelings. This does not mean, however, that there will be no areas of disagreement; but one of the objects of an appraisal interview is to see that such disagreements are dealt with and eradicated before they can become the cause of major areas of conflict.

Listen carefully to what the employee has to say, just as he must listen to you. If you have some constructive criticism to offer, then by all means mention it – but bear in mind the technique of beginning and ending with a positive statement, even if there is something negative to be said in the middle.

7. Full Discussion

During your discussions try to cover all aspects of the job so that, when the interview comes to an end, each party knows precisely where he (or she) stands. While you may be mentioning areas where improvement is thought to be needed, be sure to pass on your positive views too, as nothing will be gained if the employee ends up so demoralized that he either thinks he will never succeed or else decides to leave the company altogether.

It is only by motivating the appraisee and generating in him a sense of enthusiasm that you will get the type of response you are seeking.

When this part of the discussion comes to an end, sum up what has been said and any conclusions which may have been reached – and, indeed, any areas of disagreement which still exist. In this way the employee will be left in no doubt as to what has been achieved so far.

Once this has been done, discussion should proceed to future courses of action – and this should be done in such a way that the employee ends up actively anxious to get on with the job and make a success of it.

8. Getting Feedback

When you have both had the opportunity to put your views about possible future changes, it is time to ask the appraisee how he perceives his future so far as the job is concerned. He should be encouraged to set goals and make plans, and these should be as precise as possible in the short term.

Keep your questions open rather than asking those which require a simple 'yes' or 'no' response. This will stimulate two-way conversation and you will both have an opportunity to discuss the future and work together towards formulating an appropriate strategy.

9. Appraisal Form – Part Two

Complete Part Two of the appraisal form in the presence of the employee, ensuring that you agree on what is written there. Then each of you should sign the completed form (Parts One and Two). One copy should be retained for your records, the other given to the appraisee himself.

A Typical Appraisal Form

PART ONE

Name:

Position in company:

Length of time in that position:

Length of time with company:

Work Assessment

On a scale of 1 to 10, grade level of achievement
in tasks or projects to date:

Description of project (1):
Grade:
Comments:

Description of project (2):
Grade:
Comments:

Description of project (3):
Grade:
Comments:

Description of project (4):
Grade:
Comments:

Personal Skills

Compatibility with other team members
Grade:
Comments:

Communication skills
Grade:
Comments:

Time-management skills
Grade:
Comments:

PART TWO

How do you feel about your own job performance?
Grade:
Comments:

What is your level of job satisfaction?
Grade:
Comments:

How do you feel about your personal skills?
Grade:
Comments:

What are your personal goals:
1. Short term (6–12 months):
2. Long term (more than 12 months):
Comments:

What changes will be needed if these goals are to be achieved?
Comments:

What training or guidance do you feel will be needed if these goals are to be achieved?
Comments:

Signed by
Appraiser ....
Appraisee ....
Date:

Analysing the Appraisal

As both the appraiser and the employee will have a copy of the appraisal form after the interview, each will have the opportunity to analyse what is written there and the facts which gave rise to those comments.

It is often surprising how someone who works quite closely with another person and feels that he knows and understands the other person quite well may actually not know anything about how the other person thinks.

Here are some tips for analysing an appraisal effectively:

THE APPRAISER

- You will now have a good idea of the employee's opinion of how well he (or she) has been doing the job until now. If this opinion differs greatly from your own, you need to consider how this conflict of opinion has arisen. Once you have worked this out, if it is something which was not covered during the appraisal itself you must set about putting things right so that each of you has a clear, genuine and consistent view of recent progress and achievements.

- It may be that, even though the employee's work is entirely satisfactory, his interpersonal skills leave something to be desired. Don't overlook this as it can be the cause of friction and conflict within a team.

- Now that you know his long-term aims and ambitions, you will be able to bear him in mind whenever a suitable post comes along.

- You should be able to formulate future training plans for your team – particularly once you have conducted several appraisal interviews.

- If a specific grievance concerning work is put forward by several appraisees, you will know that you need to do something about it. Perhaps it will be a situation you can deal with personally. If not, and if those in a superior position to you need to intervene, remember that, while it may be necessary to pass on information about this grievance, confidentiality should be

respected and the names of those who put forward the grievances should not be mentioned, unless they request this.

THE APPRAISEE

- The appraisee will benefit from having a greater understanding of how he is seen by others, both in regard to his work
abilities and to his interpersonal skills. If he is taken by sur-
prise by some of these opinions, this will give him the opportunity to decide whether he wants to make changes and, if he
does, to consider how to go about it.

- Having discussed long-term goals and aims with the appraiser, the employee should have a fair idea of whether he is
likely to be encouraged towards them. He will be able to base
future plans on the outcome of those discussions.

- If his skills are to be encouraged, the employee should be
aware that future training is likely and, indeed, he may be able
to request it in specific areas.

Formal appraisals of this sort are comparatively new in the world
of business. Provided they are treated correctly and positively,
the results can only enhance the performance of both the company and the individuals who work for it.

CHAPTER TEN

Discipline

One part of their job that most managers or supervisors really dislike is having to discipline members of their staff. This is understandable – particularly if the supervisor has been appointed from the ranks and is having to deal with those who were previously her (or his) fellow workers. Yet if discipline is not enforced and maintained, conflicts which could have started as minor incidents will not only persist but will probably escalate – often out of all reasonable proportions. It is not unknown for such conflicts to develop into destructive situations which feed so greatly on themselves that the original cause of grievance or dissatisfaction is actually forgotten.

It is important for every manager or supervisor to remember that everything done by her team will reflect directly upon her. And this applies to the bad as well as the good. If the work output is of poor standard or if there is seen to be general disharmony within the team, you can be sure that the manager will be made aware of the disapproval of her own superiors. By disciplining the employee(s) concerned, she will be shifting the balance of blame to where it belongs.

The greatest problems arise when the manager/supervisor has not been adequately trained in methods of disciplining staff and dealing with problems. It may be only simple constructive and well-intentioned criticism which is needed or it may be a full-scale disciplinary interview or even an official hearing. If you feel that you have not been adequately taught to deal with this type of situation, it is up to you to request further training. Very few companies will refuse as it is obviously in their own best interests to have on their staff someone who is able to solve situations and deal with problems of discipline before major conflicts arise within the organization.

When an internal problem arises within your team, don't immediately conclude that what is needed is a full-scale formal manager's disciplinary interview. That should only be used as a last resort. In many instances you will be able to settle minor conflicts in their very early stages, thus finding solutions to the problems created by poor workmanship or difficulties within the personal relationships of members of your team – whether these relationships are work-related or private ones.

If there is perceived to be a problem, the employees concerned must always be made officially aware of it. They should also be informed as to what they are expected to do about it – as well as what are likely to be the consequences if they do not.

One of the reasons the supervisor might hesitate before disciplining employees is that she fears that team atmosphere might be destroyed by her actions. She may anticipate being on the receiving end of resentment or even hostility. This, however, is extremely unlikely. What is far more likely to happen is that she will, in fact, gain the respect of the rest of her team and then, provided the matter is dealt with once and for all and then ignored, it is possible that even the disciplined employees will come to respect her as they realize that they cannot get away with what they formerly did.

Catherine worked as part of a team in a large technical design company. All her colleagues were men and several were somewhat older than she was. When the team supervisor was promoted, his position became vacant and the company management decided to offer Catherine the opportunity to fill it. This she did with a mixture of pride for having been selected and some trepidation because she was unsure how this rise in status would be regarded by her colleagues.

At first she did encounter a certain amount of resentment – in particular from those who had been in a similar position with the organization for several years and therefore believed that they had far more knowledge than she did. There was also some thinly-veiled hostility from one or two of the more chauvinistic members of the team.

Catherine took all this in her stride and, because she was an assertive – although not aggressive – person, she soon began to win over this all-male group of former colleagues. They could certainly find no fault with her work or her administrative abilities and she had a firm but gentle way of instilling them with her own enthusiasm about new projects.

In fact, about three months after being promoted Catherine told me that she was enjoying her new position and status and that the only difficulty she felt was a certain amount of embarrassment on Friday evenings. For as long as the team had worked together, it had been their habit to go out for a drink after leaving work on a Friday evening. Although not a great drinker, Catherine had always accompanied them and had enjoyed their outings. After her promotion she was unsure whether to continue to join her male colleagues or whether to make her way quietly home. The situation was solved for her when one of the younger men made a point of reminding her that it was Friday and that they had arranged to try a different pub for their regular weekly drink. From that time onwards she had always joined them and, after a certain amount of teasing about her new position, had been able to settle down into a friendly routine during this out-of-work activity without feeling that it undermined her authority in the workplace.

Catherine's first major problem arose when it came to her attention that James, one of her team, was (apparently deliberately) causing friction within the team, as a result of which everyone's work was suffering. James was about 15 years her senior and had been with the company some five years longer than she had; indeed, he had been one of those showing most resentment when Catherine was first promoted.

Catherine knew that she had to do something about the situation before matters became worse, but she hesitated in case it appeared that she was exacting some sort of petty revenge for the earlier antagonistic attitude James had shown towards her. It was then that the isolation of her position struck her: she could not seek advice from those who had formerly been her peers and she felt that, if she approached her own supervisors, it might seem that she was not capable of doing the job to which they had promoted her.

For a while Catherine did nothing – hoping, perhaps, that the problem would magically disappear. But of course it did not. Not only that but, like any problem which is not dealt with, it grew worse. Finally she decided that, whatever her team thought of her, she would have to do something about James. So she set up a meeting with him at which she calmly but firmly explained that she was aware of the situation and that he was the cause, and she would not permit it to continue. She set out exactly what changes she expected to see if matters were not to be taken further.

James did not say a great deal at the time but his behaviour changed noticeably over the following days and weeks – much to Catherine's relief. Not only that, but she became aware that her team were now treating her with more respect than previously and that both the atmosphere and the work output had improved considerably.

In this chapter we are dealing with discipline in the form of the conflict-solving interview rather than with the legal requirements of formal disciplinary hearings and tribunals, the rules and procedures of which are more rigid and more complicated. After all, if the supervisor is aware enough of situations around her, in many cases problems can be solved before the need for more formal disciplinary hearings arises.

Having made that point, it is wise to keep full contemporary records of any interviews and meetings, however informal, in case matters need to be taken further at a later date.

Although we have seen that disciplinary interviews are necessary and indeed beneficial, it is not usually a good idea to react instantly when you first become aware of a problem which needs handling in this way. There are two main reasons for this:

1) You need time to check all details and facts before making any accusatory remarks. This may involve a considerable amount of investigation and possible involvement of other people – who will also have to be sure of what they are saying. In some cases, you may discover that there has been a misunderstanding; in some, another person may have been maliciously and deliberately misleading you; in others, the matter will turn out to be fairly trivial and one which can perhaps be dealt with on a more casual basis, avoiding the need for a disciplinary interview altogether.

2) Because nothing is ever gained by taking action when tempers are high, time must be allowed for everyone to cool off. It is not only your own temper which needs time to abate, but that of the employee concerned and of anyone else who may be involved in the situation with which you have to deal.

If, after this cooling-off period, you are convinced that it is necessary to go ahead with a disciplinary interview, the employee concerned should always be notified in writing of this fact. As well as the time and place of the interview itself, she (or he) should be made aware of the reasons for it so that she has time to collect her own thoughts and collate any information which may be in support of her actions.

The Interview

During the interview itself, it is up to the supervisor to give the employee a full and detailed explanation of what is expected of her (or him) if she is to fulfil the role in which she is employed within the organization. Having done that, even if written on her notification of the date and time of the interview the employee must be told about the way in which she has failed to meet those expectations.

This applies whether the problem which has arisen is task related or whether it concerns the behaviour or attitude of the employee. She should then be asked:

A) whether she understands what has been said to her
B) whether or not she accepts the truth of the comments made to her about her problems
C) to give an explanation for the problems if possible; or to tell her side of the story, should her viewpoint be different.

Whatever her response, the supervisor should give her both time and attention. Try to hear her out without interrupting. Depending upon the nature of the individual concerned, she may be good at giving her side of the story – or she may not. So give her ample time to refute what has been alleged if appropriate and to make any comments of her own that she may wish to make. Let your body language show that you are listening and taking in what she is saying, even while you are not speaking.

As the supervisor/manager – and therefore the person who is really in charge of the situation – you will find that you have to deal with many different types of personalities in this sort of situation. Some people, when confronted with their own short-comings, say little or nothing in response. But it is important that you manage to hear their opinions. This is partly because there may be some genuine underlying problem of which you are unaware and which may alter your perspective on the situation, and partly because it is possible that, even if the employee says nothing during the interview, she may feel at a later date that she wishes to take the matter further and may take advice on doing so. If this should happen, it is important that you are *seen* to have given her every opportunity to put forward her side of the story.

In order to encourage the employee to speak, make sure that you use open questions (those which cannot be answered with a simple 'yes' or 'no').

If the employee appears to have a tendency to stray from the subject – whether deliberately or accidentally – it is up to you, gently but firmly, to bring her back to it. Thereafter you must do what you can to keep her to the point being discussed.

Sometimes, of course, the employee may raise a point in her own defence or in mitigation of her actions of which you had no former knowledge. Or you might reach a stage at which it becomes obvious that your point of view and hers are diametrically opposed to one another. Should this arise, listen carefully to what the employee says, taking notes if necessary, and promise to check on the situation and get back to her. It is essential that you keep this promise if you are not to lose her trust and respect.

Perhaps this is an instance where, in spite of the views and opinions of others, the employee genuinely believes that she is in the right and has acted accordingly.

Should such a situation arise there are a few pertinent questions you should ask yourself:

- Do the company rules fit the current situation?
- If they do, are you certain that they were made clear to the employee from the very beginning? If they were not, perhaps some further training is needed either on the part of the original communicator or of the employee herself?
- If those rules were made clear at the outset and yet the employee has either forgotten them or did not think they applied in the case in question, should there be some kind of gentle reminder issued from time to time so that no one can claim ignorance of a particular set of rules?

If the problem is one of attitude or behaviour rather than of standard of work, you will need to discover as much as you can about the interpersonal relationships within your team. This may well require further investigation on your part.

Perhaps the employee has a particular home-related personal problem about which she has not spoken but which may well be affecting both her temper and her behaviour towards others. If she has, it may hopefully come to the fore during the course of the interview. If that happens you may of course decide that assistance rather than discipline is what is needed – provided the employee is willing to accept help. You will then have to decide whether you are personally capable of rendering this assistance or whether it would be better for the employee to be referred to a professional counsellor.

When dealing with a member of your team who has a personal problem, you cannot hope to solve the problem for her (or him). Whether the matter is handled by you or by a professionally trained counsellor, the best that can be done is to show the employee how she can learn to overcome her own problems.

In this sort of situation it may be necessary to explain to other team members any relaxation of rules in favour of this particular employee. You cannot, of course, betray her confidence by explaining what her problem is but, provided you have a good working relationship with your team, they should trust you sufficiently well to realize that you must have a good reason for any concessions you do make.

The best possible outcome of a disciplinary interview is that both supervisor and employee find a point of agreement about what has been going wrong and what can be done about it. These points should be written down at the time of the interview and signed by both parties, who will then have a copy each. This prevents any conflict arising at a later date because of either deliberate misrepresentation or a lapse in memory by either or both.

As soon as the interview has been concluded, the supervisor should write a report of what took place; this should be kept on file in case the matter arises again some time in the future.

The importance of writing this report *immediately* after the interview cannot be stressed enough. We all like to think that we have good memories, but it is so easy to change a nuance or to miss out a fact altogether – without ever intending to do so – that the sooner the report is written the better it is for all concerned.

Daunting as the prospect of a disciplinary interview may appear, most end quite satisfactorily provided there is a reasonable element of co-operation between supervisor and employee. Naturally, no one is happy to be on the receiving end of criticism – whether or not it is justified – so, even though you should not hold back from expressing criticism where it is needed, make sure that you do so in as assertive and constructive a way as possible.

Criticism

All criticism should be factual rather than judgemental. While you may have to say to someone 'you are frequently late,' you do not have the right to add 'you're hopeless' or 'you're lazy'. (If the lateness of the employee is an issue of the disciplinary interview, it should be backed up with dates, times, etc.)

Criticism should also be able to lead on to constructive suggestions. Obviously, in the case of lateness, the aim would be that this should cease. This point should be made clear to the employee, who must then be given the chance to make any comment.

For example, in one case that I know of the employee was a single mother with a disabled son. The child attended a special day centre, and was taken there by his mother before she came to work each morning. Sometimes this caused her to be late. Because she had not told her supervisor about these domestic arrangements concerning her son, it appeared that this employee was just a bad time-keeper and she was summoned to an interview to discuss this.

At the interview the situation was explained in full and, because of the special circumstances, the supervisor was able to 'bend the rules' and make allowances for the woman's frequent lateness. With the employee's permission, the matter was also explained to her colleagues so that they would not feel resentful if they saw her getting what might seem to be special treatment.

Points to Bear in Mind during a Disciplinary Interview

Keep to the Point

Base the interview on the current situation and what has occurred recently – all of which should have been contained in the notification of the interview sent or given to the employee in advance. It may be tempting – particularly if you feel the employee is trying to justify her actions when she has little cause to do so – to bring into the matter her behaviour last year, what other people have done in the past or what happens in other companies. None of this has any relevance and can only lead to confusion or to a distortion of the current facts.

Stay Calm

Whatever happens, and however difficult a personality the employee may turn out to be, *never* allow yourself to lose your temper. Anyone who is the least bit perceptive – whether consciously or subconsciously – will soon pick up on this as a sign of outer aggression hiding inner weakness, and will play on that fact.

By all means let your verbal and body language be assertive at all times, but don't be tempted to stray into the realm of aggression. This applies in all cases but is particularly important if the employee happens to be an aggressive person herself. In such a case, were you to lose your temper too, all you would end up with would be a shouting match which would serve no useful purpose and would result in you losing both the employee's respect and your own.

Keep your manner friendly. Even though this may be a disciplinary interview it should be conducted in as positive a way as possible. The idea is not to concentrate on recriminations about the past but to decide together what needs to be done differently in the future and to come to an agreement about how this is to be achieved.

Make Sure the Employee Stays Calm Too

Some people are naturally aggressive – but you will already be aware that this is an indication of their inner insecurity. Some, who are otherwise quite mild, will automatically react aggressively if they feel that they are being put under pressure. Others will deliberately adopt the policy of 'attack being the most effective form of defence' when they are criticized.

Whatever the reason for a display of temper, you must put an end to it as soon as it starts. Often the easiest way of stopping someone who is in full aggressive flow is to say her name firmly (but without shouting). You may even have to repeat it several times – but it works. Imagine being faced with a man who has lost control of his temper and who does not cease his tirade to listen to your point of view. If you say to him, 'Matthew. Matthew' – then, once you have his attention, 'Let's just discuss this calmly, shall we?' You will find, in the majority of cases, that this is all it takes to prevent a serious escalation of verbal hostility.

Remain Firm

Because you are not going to allow yourself to become aggressive, this does not mean that you are going to be weak or ineffectual. You will have had time to consider the particular situation before the time of the interview, so you will know what changes you deem to be necessary in order to improve the situation. If the employee has not been able to persuade you that you are wrong – if she has been able to, you may need to make new decisions – then you must firmly state what these changes are to be. It is then up to the employee to indicate whether or not she is willing to make those changes, how she intends to go about it and what her views are about the situation. If there is any hesitation on her part, you have the right to point out to her the likely consequences for her of not making the changes as requested.

Keep All Questions Open-ended

This is intended to be a forum for discussion – which implies a two-way conversation. Some people, when faced with a difficult situation, will simply clam up and say nothing at all. This may be because they know they are in the wrong and they don't know how to get out of it, because they are extremely nervous, or because they think that, if they say nothing, the situation will go away of its own accord.

If you are conducting this interview, what you need is to get the employee to speak so that the desired discussion can taken place. If your questions are closed and merit only a 'yes' or 'no' answer, this is all they are likely to receive. This will not help the progress of the discussion in any way. Open-ended questions, such as 'What is your opinion of...?', 'How do you think this problem arose?' or 'What suggestions can you make for future improvement?' compel the employee to speak.

If all you get in response to your questions is a mumbled 'don't know', you will have to force the issue by asking the employee to think about it and give you her answer.

If the employee still says nothing (hoping that you will speak again in order to break the silence), you must remain silent too. This is actually quite difficult if you find yourself in such a situation. The silence can seem endless, and a few seconds may feel like half an hour. But remember that this is probably what the employee is relying on, so don't give in. If it gets to the stage where you really cannot bear the silence any longer or where you think the employee really is not going to speak at all, put her on the spot by saying something like, 'Well?' or 'I really need to hear your answer' and then be silent once more. Eventually she will have to speak to you.

Because the reason behind some people's silence is that they are extremely nervous – particularly when faced with a disciplinary interview – make sure that you maintain positive and friendly body language while waiting for the employee to speak.

Don't Jump to Conclusions

If any point arises during the interview about which you are not sure, it is far better to say so than to make assumptions based on what you already know. Should these assumptions turn out to be false, you will lose all credibility regarding not just these assumptions but also anything else which has arisen during the interview. An assertive person is one who wants a situation in which everyone is a winner; she (or he) is therefore not afraid to say that there is something she is not sure of. What is important at that point is to add that you will make investigations about the area of uncertainty – and then to do so, letting the employee know the results of any enquiries you make.

Avoid Personal Insults

Whatever your opinion of the individual with whom you are dealing during the interview – and whatever that person's own behaviour – there is never any excuse for sinking to the level of hurling personal insults at each other. There may be times – hopefully not too frequently – when you may have your patience sorely tried, but you cannot afford to lower the tone of the interview in this way.

Agreement

Before the interview comes to an end, make sure that an agreement has been reached about desired changes and how they are to be achieved. Once written down, these should be read and agreed by both parties to avoid confusion or disagreement in the future.

Putting the Past Behind You

Once the interview has been completed, and provided the employee changes in whatever way has been agreed between you, it is up to you to ensure that the matter is put behind you and that you do not refer to it in the future. Nor should you be seen to treat that employee any differently from anyone else on the team.

CHAPTER ELEVEN

Negotiation

Negotiation is all around us in life. It is present when we settle on the price of an item at a car boot sale; it exists when we agree with a teenage son what time he should come home from a party; it is there when we decide with friend or partner upon a film we would both like to watch.

We have all been negotiating in one way or another all our lives without thinking anything of it. And yet, when we hear the word 'negotiation' in relation to the business environment we immediately tend to think in terms of arguments, demands and concessions.

Similarly, compromise is not a dirty word. It does not imply that there is a victor and a vanquished. It simply means that two or more people have come to an arrangement which satisfies them all, even though no one may have achieved every one of his or her desired aims.

Negotiation is actually a highly assertive and very valuable business skill. It is a method of discussion and interaction which enables two or more parties, each with their own aims and desired outcomes, to come together to a satisfactory conclusion – one which is to everyone's greatest possible advantage.

The outcome of successful negotiation is a win/win situation which results in all parties being content. It does not involve one party or group of people taking unfair advantage of the other or using devious methods because they are determined to get their own way no matter who else suffers in the process.

In business it may be necessary to negotiate quality, deadlines and costs with a supplier or with a customer. When dealing with the workforce it may be a case of negotiating with regard to pay, to hours, to starting or finishing times or to productivity. Negotiations with the accounts department might take place in order to increase the funding for a particular job or department.

When dealing with an existing or a potential conflict situation, it may be necessary to assist negotiations between several parties. You might be an actual participant in the conflict or you might be using your position as supervisor or manager to resolve a conflict between two or more members of your team.

If asked, most people would say that they do not like the thought of having to become involved in negotiations. They give many different reasons for this, the most common being:

- They think that, because compromise is obviously going to be involved, everyone will end up being dissatisfied with the outcome and so it seems that a great deal of effort only results in a great deal of discontent.
- They feel that, particularly if they are confronted with what seems like stubbornness from the other party, they might lose their temper and say things they regret. Only the truly aggressive person does not mind losing his (or her) temper – and such as person is so insensitive that he will never be prepared to negotiate anyway. Most everyone else, whether they admit it publicly or not, feels that they have let themselves down if they lose their temper – and this is a feeling no one enjoys.

    Of course, it may be that they fear an explosion of rage on the part of the other person and do not wish to have to deal with this. However, if negotiations are conducted properly and in the right spirit, there should be no need for anyone on either side to lose control.
- They fear losing the friendship and respect of the other party if they appear either too tough when it comes to the negotiations or not tough enough. This fear stems from a misunderstanding of what negotiating is and the best way of going about it.

- It is too time-consuming. Of course it would be far quicker just to tell someone what you want him to do. But that would only be the case in the short term. In the long term such a 'solution' would not only antagonize the other party (because it would seem so uncompromising), it would probably result in battles over each and every point of possible conflict in the future and much more time would have to be given up to negotiations of a different sort.
- They would feel humiliated if they were to 'lose'. This shows a misunderstanding of true negotiation, where there are no losers – only parties who have reached an agreement with which they are all satisfied – and after which there is no need for anyone to feel humiliated.
- They do not like upsetting other people or hurting their feelings. Once again, if negotiations are conducted properly this possibility should not arise. If someone is sensitive enough not to want to upset anyone else, he (or she) is certainly sensitive enough to employ proper negotiating skills and to reach an amicable compromise.

Changing the Language?

Perhaps it is easier to see negotiation for what it is if we change the language most commonly associated with it.

So, let's do away with 'opponents', replacing them with 'counterparts' or even, bearing in mind that the hoped-for outcome is a win/win situation, 'partners'.

The 'differences' which form the basic cause for the negotiation in the first place should become 'starting-points', implying that each party will end up in a different position from the one in which he begins.

The word 'argument' creates in the mind a sense of opposition and a conflict of wills. 'Discussion', however, is a more assertive and therefore a more positive way of looking at the same exchange of views.

If you feel that it is all too easy for 'negotiation' to imply eventual 'victory' for one party and 'defeat' for the other, try looking on the final outcome as an 'agreement' instead.

Consider the two statements which follow and ask yourself how you feel upon reading each one:

1) *The two opponents met last Wednesday to sort out their differences. This they did after a session of prolonged arguments which resulted in a victory for Peter and a defeat for Paul.*
2) *The two counterparts met last Wednesday to find a solution to the problem. Although their starting-points seemed far apart, after a series of discussions they were able to come to a mutual agreement.*

The two sentences are in essence describing the same event: two parties meeting to discuss a situation on which they did not initially agree, and reaching a point of compromise which satisfies them both. But the widely varying ways in which this could be articulated show how our perceptions of an event can be influenced by the language used to describe it.

Setting Limits

Think of the situation that arises when someone is buying or selling a house. The vendor may decide, before putting the house on the market, that he (or she) is prepared to accept £78,000, as this is what will be needed to enable him to purchase the property he wants. Having done that, he will usually put it on the market at £80,000 or even £85,000 in order to leave room for negotiation.

The prospective purchaser comes along to see the house. Now, in his mind he knows that the maximum he can afford to pay is £80,000. He inspects the property, decides that he likes it and would like to buy it and then he puts in an offer of, perhaps, £75,000.

Then negotiations begin. The vendor rejects the purchaser's offer and says, perhaps, that he is willing to come down by £1,000. The purchaser says that this is still too high a price, but makes a slightly higher offer than his initial one. Eventually one of two things happens: either a price is reached which satisfies both the vendor and purchaser, or it becomes apparent that there is no compromise price which fulfils the criteria each has set.

In this situation each person knows his limits before negotiations begin, and each is prepared to be flexible only within those limits. So it is in business. There will be some areas where compromise is simply not an option. Such situations include:

- where company procedure is strictly laid down and there is no room for negotiation
- where one party does not have the authority to negotiate alone and has to seek permission or advice from those in a more senior position
- where certain behaviour is concerned which is totally unacceptable and therefore not suitable for negotiation – such as racism, sexual harassment, etc.

Before Negotiations Begin

Prior to the commencement of discussion sessions, take the time to work out your position – and also, as far as possible, that of your counterpart.

There are various aspects to consider:

- The desired outcome: What would you really like to achieve and what would, from your point of view, be an ideal result?
- The acceptable outcome: The minimum you would be prepared to accept. This applies equally whether we are talking about a sum of money, an aspect of behaviour or the supply of goods.
- Boundaries: There are likely to be areas where compromise is not an option, and these should be at the forefront of your mind before negotiations begin.
- Time limit: This does not always apply, but may be relevant in some cases – especially where the exchange of money for goods or services, or a change in a particular individual's

behaviour, is concerned.

- Back-up: It is important to have at your fingertips any facts or resources which may help to sway the discussions in your favour.
- Temptations: Do you have anything specific you can offer your counterpart which is likely to make him more amenable to an early compromise?

Although you may not know precisely what is in the mind of your counterpart, you will probably have a fairly good idea. Being as realistic as possible, consider the following:

- Desired outcome: This is something you are likely to know because it forms the basis for the discussion in the first place.
- Acceptable outcome: What do you think is likely to be the minimum he will accept?
- Limitations: Does he have areas where he is likely to be adamant about what he wants and where the option of compromise cannot be considered?
- Resources: What facts and resources is he likely to arm himself with and how influential would they be in swaying your opinion?
- Temptation: Is there anything he could put on the table which would be so tempting to you that you would be prepared to alter your original position?

Personal Attitude

Your attitude of mind before entering into negotiations of any sort is very important.

You are not going into battle. It is quite possible that in any negotiation each party feels he is right and that he has what he sees as perfectly valid reasons for holding out for what he wants. You need to think in terms of your counterpart's aims and desires as well as your own.

This is a time to be as truly assertive as possible and to start from the position where you accept that the probable outcome is one of compromise – and that there is nothing wrong with this. Provided you do not overstep the boundaries you set for yourself, it is more important to concentrate on achieving an outcome with which everyone can be content than being a winner yourself.

Be as positive as you can from the outset so that your counterpart realizes that you are not his enemy but that you are seeking an area within which you can come together.

Dale Carnegie in *How to Win Friends and Influence People* writes of 'talking in terms of the other person's interests'. In other words, the more you can put forward your ideas as ways in which your counterpart is likely to benefit, the more probable it is that you will persuade him over to your side sooner rather than later.

If you are asking for something, be ready with an offer in return before the other person demands it. For example, suppose you have an urgent document which needs typing but it is late in the afternoon and you know your secretary likes to leave at five o'clock. Which of the following is most likely to persuade him to stay late and help you out?

1. Mr Jones, I need this document on my desk first thing in the morning. You'll have to stay on this evening and type it.

2. Mr Jones, I have an important meeting at nine o'clock tomorrow and this document is really urgent. I realize you like to leave at five but, if you could help me by staying a little later to type it for me, you needn't come in until noon tomorrow.

Mr Jones probably doesn't want to stay late but he will find it far harder to refuse if you show him that you realize this, appreciate that you are imposing on him and are willing to show your gratitude by giving him some time off in lieu.

Handling Negotiations
between Yourself and Another Person

Don't Rush Things

Haste can be your greatest enemy. Take your time before even beginning discussions to analyse your own and your counterpart's position as illustrated earlier in this chapter.

It is even a good idea to slow down the rate at which you speak during the actual negotiations. For one thing this has the effect of making you sound much wiser and more sure of yourself (try it and see). Anyone who speaks rapidly gives the impression of being either nervous or more aggressive than he might actually be. For another thing, it gives you the opportunity to think as you go and, therefore, to take into consideration whatever your counterpart has to say and what would be the best response. Slower speech will also have the effect of making the other person more inclined to stop and listen to you, because you will sound as though you need to be taken very seriously.

Help Your Counterpart Feel Good about Himself

No great compromise was ever achieved by one person making the other feel inferior. It would be possible in such a situation to get your own way – particularly if you were in a position of seniority – but that is not a satisfactory solution. It might mean that you achieve what you want in the short term, but you will have alienated your counterpart – possibly for ever – and this can cause you even greater problems should the need arise for future negotiations.

So listen carefully to what he (or she) has to say. Even if you do not agree with him, indicate by your words that you *understand* his viewpoint and appreciate that he holds a sincere opinion.

Leave Room for Negotiation

There is little point in beginning the discussion by stating what you want and indicating that you are unwilling to deviate one iota from that point.

If you realize that there is an area of difference between you, start from a point which allows you space to negotiate – and does the same for your counterpart. In this way no one will feel that he has been browbeaten into submission.

Persuade Your Counterpart to Begin the Discussion

Many of us believe that we know what another person wants, yet we may be mistaken. It is so easy to make assumptions because of hearsay, previous experience or your own attitude. By allowing the other person to open the discussion, you may in fact find that he is nearer to you than you had expected and that you do not, therefore, have to deviate as far from your own desires as you had previously expected to do.

Don't Give in Too Quickly

Although no one wants discussions to go on for ever, it is none the less worth taking the time to iron out every possible area of negotiation. This prevents misunderstandings between you and your counterpart. It also provides a little extra time for the possibility that he might move one step nearer to your own point of view – for the sake of a few extra minutes you might achieve more than you would otherwise have done.

Say No Where Essential

We looked earlier at areas where compromise is just not possible. These areas should be made clear to your counterpart in a firm but friendly way, so that he knows precisely where he stands and does not mistake this for yet another area where discussion might lead you to change your mind.

Remember that negotiation, compromise and the win/win situation are closely linked to assertive behaviour. Remember too that one of the things an assertive person is able to do is to say no when necessary.

Keep It Friendly

However far apart the views of you and your counterpart may be at the beginning, never allow the discussion to deteriorate into the realm of personal judgement or insult. There is nothing to be gained by telling the other person that he is 'stupid' or 'ignorant'. Such comments – or even an attitude which suggests that you feel this way – will only increase the conflict and reduce the likelihood of any successful outcome to your discussions.

Acting as Mediator

What we have been dealing with so far are the techniques and aspects of relatively formal negotiations where two or more people come together with the aim of reaching a point of agreement. There are, however, likely to be occasions when you will be called upon to help two or more others reach a state of compromise – in other words, to act as mediator when a conflict situation exists.

This applies particularly when there is no clear-cut 'right' and 'wrong' in the situation. Obviously, if a single individual is creating difficulties or is breaking the rules in some way, then what is needed is not negotiation but some form of discipline. In many cases, however, what exists is a difference of opinion or the breakdown of a particular relationship between two or more members of your team.

In such circumstances you will probably feel that a formal interview is not the most appropriate way of sorting the matter out. What is needed here is very similar to a family therapy session. This leads not only to the clearing of the air over the existing problem but an improved relationship between those concerned in the future – thus reducing the likelihood of something similar occurring at a later date.

As soon as you are aware that there is a conflict which needs to be dealt with, arrange with the people concerned that they should join you in your office for a meeting. They should be informed of the reason for the meeting in advance so that each has time to formulate his (or her) ideas and consider any points he may wish to raise during the course of it.

(There might, of course, be any number of people concerned in a particular conflict but, for the sake of this example, let's assume that there are two – Simon and Paula.)

If the conflict has been going on for some time, the atmosphere at the meeting might be somewhat bitter or icy initially. No matter how Simon and Paula are behaving, you must remain assertive at all times. You should show, by your words, expression and body language, that you are in a positive frame of mind and that you are equally well disposed towards both of them. If this session is to work, it is vital that neither Simon nor Paula feels that you are taking sides or trying to force a resolution of the problem upon them.

It is as well to keep this session as informal as possible, so try and arrange for comfortable chairs to be available; perhaps a cup of tea or coffee will help to break the ice.

You should begin by stating that you are aware that there is some sort of problem being encountered by the two of them with regard to each other. Let them know that the sole purpose of the meeting is to sort out the problem, reach a conclusion which is satisfactory to both of them, and lay the foundations for a happier relationship between them in the future.

Next you need to set out the ground rules for the meeting. Both Simon and Paula will have ample opportunity to put their views, but they will do this one at a time – and they will address all comments to *you* and not to each other. You promise them that each will have the chance to say whatever he or she wishes, but that you will not tolerate raised voices or other signs of aggression.

You also need to let them know that you will not be 'making

a ruling' but are there as a facilitator to help them reach a 'mutually agreeable solution'.

Now, beginning with one of them – let's suppose it is Paula. Ask her to tell you what she feels to be the core of the problem which exists between her and Simon. Simon must remain silent while she speaks – interruptions are not allowed even if he feels that Paula is misrepresenting the situation.

You then ask Simon what he feels the problem to be and what his reaction is to Paula's introductory words.

And so the meeting goes on, each person being given the chance to speak without being interrupted and to respond to what the other person has just said. Your task, in addition to keeping the peace and keeping both parties fixed on the subject being dealt with, is to establish the following points:

1) What does each of them see as the existing problem?
2) How do they think the original problem arose?
3) What would be the best outcome from their personal point of view?
4) What would be the very least they would accept?
5) In what way would they be prepared to compromise to achieve a mutually satisfactory outcome?

Then, although you will not be a negotiator yourself, you guide them through the negotiating process until a compromise is reached. At no point should you allow the conversation to deteriorate to the level of personal attacks or irrelevant judgemental remarks.

Once a compromise has been reached, adopt similar tactics to establish what Simon and Paula want for the future and how they intend to ensure that a similar situation does not arise again.

The interesting thing about meetings of this sort is that, in many cases, the 'adversaries' turn out not to be so far apart from each other after all. You will frequently find that either:

- each has been labouring under a misunderstanding about the other person's point of view, or:
- tempers have become raised so that bitter words (or no words at all) have been exchanged which have hidden the real problem.

Training

It is generally accepted these days in most companies that training is beneficial. Unfortunately, that training still seems to consist mostly of the more obviously practical skills as opposed to the human resource ones. So there may be ample training in handling a computer, closing a sale or caring for customers – but very little on personal skills such as assertiveness, communication or managing stress.

Perhaps the reason for ignoring such vital areas is that those controlling a company's finances cannot always see the benefits of spending money on personal skills training. If they buy a new piece of equipment, there it is gleaming and ready to use. If they train the sales force in effective sales techniques, they can measure any beneficial outcome by keeping an eye on the sales figures. But improving the human relations skills of their workforce may not produce tangible benefits for quite some time. But it is obvious that a happier team of people is going to take a greater interest in their work and therefore achieve more in the end. There will also be far greater company loyalty because those working for it will realize that they are being treated as individuals and not as components of some giant machine.

The result of all this is that, with less stress and less conflict, you will find less absenteeism and a more enthusiastic approach to work – and therefore greater productivity.

Perhaps one could equate human resource training with having a medical check-up or servicing a car. It is hardly a good idea to wait to do either of these until your personal health or your vehicle breaks down. The ideal time for either is when all appears to be well so that (i) you can be forewarned should there be a problem on the horizon and (ii) you can have that little bit of fine-tuning which can help either you or your vehicle to perform the very peak of ability.

Given all the possible benefits, you should try to encourage the management of your company to introduce this type of training into the organization.

Mending Bridges

Whether the conflict exists between you and another person or whether you are trying to help resolve a conflict situation between members of your team, the most important thing is to get people talking. This will avoid the 'I know what he's thinking' state of affairs and will also show that you are concerned about putting matters right in whatever way possible.

Before any meeting of people who are in disagreement, try to think of something positive to say about each one – and say it. Many people find this difficult initially, but the results make it well worth while. Instead of being seen as 'the enemy' (if you are personally involved) or as a 'dictator' (if you are mediating), people will be more willing to accept that, although you may not be in agreement with them, you are not judging them as individuals.

There is an old saying that 'time heals'. Unfortunately, while this may be true in some areas of life it does not apply to resolving conflict or the ill-will it frequently creates. If you leave the situation to be dealt with by time, you will find yourself with an even greater problem on your hands. Not only will the existing conflict not be solved, but personal feelings of animosity will be bound to escalate. Thus, the Paulas and Simons may become so bitter about each other that they find themselves unconsciously looking for areas to disagree about in the future.

A Maintenance Programme

Once you have dealt with any conflict situation existing among members of your team, you will want to do your best to ensure that such problems do not arise again, for many reasons:

- They have a destructive effect on the team as a whole.
- Productivity is reduced as energies are concentrated on the conflict itself.
- Those in a higher position than you might feel that you are incapable of managing effectively.
- Dealing with conflict situations can be time- and energy-consuming.

There are, therefore, various points to bear in mind which could prevent minor difficulties escalating into major conflicts in the future:

- Be observant and do your best to deal with any situation the moment you become aware of it.
- Improve your own self-esteem so that you do not allow yourself to develop a 'victim mentality' where you feel you are being governed by the vagaries of fate or of the whims and fancies of other people.
- Boost the self-esteem of those around you. Give praise where it is due. Too many managers are ready to criticize – and there is nothing wrong with this provided the criticisms are justified and constructive. But don't forget to pay compliments as well.
- Once you have resolved a conflict situation effectively, think through all that you did, making note of what you did well and learning from areas where you think there could be some improvement.
- Consider the possibility of arranging a team forum at regular intervals. This would give everyone an opportunity to express his (or her) views in a positive way, and would make you more aware of those aspects of the team's work and working relationships with which they were happy and those which they felt could do with some improvement.

During such a forum your task would be to act as ombudsman or mediator in the way detailed above in the description of the meeting between Simon and Paula.

You might be thinking that there just is not time in your busy schedule to fit in such forum meetings at regular intervals (and 'regular' should mean monthly or even weekly). But consider the time you would have to expend on dealing with conflicts once they develop – I think you will find that such forums are a much more efficient and beneficial alternative. They also have the advantage of making each participant feel that he (or she) is important to the company, thereby increasing and improving staff loyalty.

And who knows where it could all lead? Those who see that conflict in the workplace can be solved by assertive compromise might be encouraged to put the same techniques into practice at home or even when dealing with their extended family. If the majority of families were able to resolve their differences amicably, perhaps in time this ability would spread to take in neighbourhoods, towns and even countries. Think how the world would change if we all chose negotiation over conflict?

CHAPTER TWELVE

The Complete Strategy

A Step-by-step Guide to Conflict Management

I. WHY CONFLICT ARISES

- A certain amount of conflict is bound to arise. It can be positive and helpful provided no malice or judgemental criticism is involved.
- The personalities of individuals – and their reaction to conflict – are governed to a great extent by their background, circumstances and upbringing.
- In any group of individuals in the workplace, each person has different needs, and views the job in a different light.
- Type A personalities may seem on the surface more difficult to deal with but they are often the high achievers and the people with the most innovative ideas.
- Type B personalities are less ambitious and less competitive but usually perform a given task to the best of their ability.
- The three main categories of personality are: aggressive, submissive and assertive (Type A personalities are always aggressive; Type Bs can be either assertive or submissive). The assertive personality is the one to be aimed for. Once you recognize each type, however, you can handle people in such a way that you bring out the best in them.

The aggressive person is the verbal bully who is basically insecure. He (or she) is rarely popular and can easily be the cause of conflict within a team.

The submissive person is easily put upon and can prove to

be irritating to those who have to work alongside him, thus causing friction even among those who would normally be kindly disposed towards him.

The assertive person respects himself as well as other people and shows this by positive verbal and body language. He values a situation in which everyone is a winner. In an ideal world, you would try to surround yourself with assertive people.

- Take the time to assess the personalities of those around you, using a basic assessment form.
- Sticking to a plan which does not take into account the personalities of those involved can be a strong source of conflict.

2. THE DIFFERENT TYPES OF CONFLICT

- Conflict can show itself on four different levels: within one individual, between two individuals, within a team of individuals or between two (or more) teams in the same organization.

Internal conflict can bring about a positive or a negative result. The individual concerned should be encouraged to analyse the pros and cons of what is going on inside her (or his) head.

Conflict between two individuals often arises when a minor irritation is not dealt with. Keep an eye open for a change in attitude between any two people and try to deal with the situation swiftly so that friction does not build up between them, as this may cause other people to take sides, thus spreading the conflict.

Conflict is not uncommon within a team of creative people, but it can be avoided by having *frequent, properly organized and monitored* brainstorming sessions.

When team discussions occur, ensure that everyone is involved to avoid misunderstandings arising. This also prevents 'yes-men' seeming to agree with everyone's point of view.

Although some companies actively encourage rivalry (and therefore possible conflict) between two teams within their organization, there is a danger that this sense of competition can become more important than the work in hand – possibly leading to unfair behaviour on the part of one or more individuals within a team.

- The most common reasons for conflict are: conflict of aims, conflict of ideas, conflict of attitude and conflict of behaviour.

A conflict of aims can occur when different people have different goals. Possible reasons for this are:

people being given information or instructions individually as opposed to in a group situation, with the result that they put a different interpretation on the words;
no opportunity for feedback at the outset;
some people naturally resent any sort of change – remember to talk in terms of the other person's interest;
negative attitude on the part of one or more of the people concerned.

A conflict of ideas may arise when:

differences of background cause people to place different meanings on the same words;
a new member joins an existing team, bringing in different methods and ideas.

A conflict of attitude is the most difficult to resolve, as it involves grappling with deeply-held views and convictions. There is little a team-leader or manager can do in this instance apart from trying to separate those in such conflict.
Conflict of behaviour arises when one or more of those involved behaves in a way the others find unacceptable.

- Whatever the cause, most conflicts conform to a typical four-stage cycle:

Stage One is the initial reaction, which is often one of anger or frustration;

Stage Two involves each person (or team) deciding what the problem is and what outcome they would like to see;

Stage Three occurs when each side puts a plan into action;

Stage Four is reached when a result has been achieved.

- Try to do something about any conflict at Stage Two, as it becomes far more difficult later on.
- If the conflict is not handled in time, long-term problems are likely to arise.
- Both aggressive and submissive people can create difficulties when long-term problems arise. Neither will then be of great value to an organization.
- Personal hostility (even when not concerned with work) can create great problems within the workplace.
- A manager should be approachable but firm and should never be seen to take sides.
- Try to avoid misunderstandings by giving information/explanations to the whole team at once, making allowances for the fact that some people grasp such details more quickly than others.

3. INTERNAL CONFLICT

- To deal with other people satisfactorily, it is necessary to understand yourself and develop your own self-esteem.
- Examine your own behaviour patterns and consider your best and worst qualities – taking into account both your work and personal life.
- If you feel that you are not confident, analyse why this is. What person or event in your past has caused you to lose confidence?
- Be prepared to give yourself credit when you do something well.
- Work through the steps of dealing with guilt – and then let it go.
- Make choices about your life and set goals so that you do not

just drift. Remember that it is possible for any adult to make changes within him- or herself.

- Anger is an energy which needs releasing if it is not to do you harm or result in conflict situations.
- Learn to say no.
- There are techniques for changing your life. These include:

  learning to relax;
  remembering a past success;
  visualizing your desired change;
  'talking to yourself' (positive affirmations)

  write positive statements on small 'affirmation cards' to be looked at often.

4. PREVENTING CONFLICT

- If you need to add a new member to the team, make sure you choose the person with the most appropriate personality.
- Analyse the personalities of the present team as follows:

  What are the positive and negative characteristics of each?
  What is each person's personality type?
  What is the business hierarchy?
  Do any conflicts already exist within the team?
  What was the nature of any past conflicts within the team?
  Are all team members good communicators?
  Are they better at working alone or in a group?
  How ambitious are they?

- Using your analysis, work out the best type of personality for a newcomer – someone who fits in well with those already there.
- Advertise for someone to fill the vacancy and send out application forms to respondents. Creating your own application forms is usually preferable to using 'ready-made' ones. Be sure to include questions the answers to which will tell you about the personality of the applicant.

- Select the most likely applicants for interview.
- Prepare well for the interview – environment, questions to be asked, etc.
- Make allowances for nervousness on the part of the interviewee.
- Use the eight-point interview technique.
- Ask open questions to encourage the applicant to talk. Keep your body language friendly. Be observant.
- Make notes immediately after each interview.
- Arrange a second interview if you have any doubts.
- Trust your intuition.

5. GOOD COMMUNICATION
- Written communication can be used as a back-up but is rarely sufficient on its own.
- With spoken communication, make sure you say what you really mean. Don't assume the other person will understand what you are thinking.
- Always give the other person the opportunity to give you feedback.
- Avoid communication through a third party.
- If you need to pass on information to several people, tell them all at the same time.
- People absorb information at different rates. The same person may absorb facts at varying rates depending on how he (or she) is feeling that day, what is going on at home, etc.
- Study the aids to effective communication and put them into practice whenever possible.
- In advance, work out the 'who, what, when, where and why' of the communication.
- Pay sincere compliments when applicable.
- Any criticism should be constructive and not judgemental.
- A meeting should be the right size for the information you want to impart.
- Eighty per cent of a spoken message is understood via the speaker's body language – so keep yours positive.
- You can always choose your own behaviour.

6. EMPOWERMENT

- When each member of a team is motivated, conflict is less likely to arise.
- The three principal methods of motivation are by (i) fear, (ii) incentive and (iii) attitude.

  Fear can only work in the very short term and discourages loyalty.

  Incentive is also temporarily effective, though you might be more successful in using it to empower yourself.

  Attitude motivation is the most successful of the three. It encourages each person to want to do her (or his) best.

- To encourage someone to progress, allow her to show what she can do.
- Lack of appreciation can be disempowering.
- Staff who suffer poor working conditions are unlikely to do their best.
- Supervision is acceptable but it should not become too strict or be too obvious, as either can destroy morale.
- Low rates of pay, compared to others doing similar work, will destroy the self-esteem of the individual concerned.
- Status symbols (office space, number of filing cabinets, etc.) should never be allowed to reach petty levels.
- Remember that negativity is contagious, so try and help any negative person you work with to overcome it before it spreads to the rest of the workforce.
- Take the time and trouble to show your appreciation where appropriate.
- Encourage each person to take pride in her part of the job – and in the job as a whole.
- Show concern for your team members as individuals and not just as workers.
- Delegate where possible.
- Encourage your team to deal well with change, and help those who feel a natural resistance to it.
- Involve your team in brainstorming sessions.

7. CONFLICT-CAUSING PERSONALITIES

Some of the most common (described in black-and-white terms) are:

the aggressor
the passive aggressor
the chronic absentee
the person who makes too many errors
negative people; these can be aggressively negative or
    depressive/negative people
the chatterbox
the do-nothing
the unreliable person
the time-waster
the resentful person.

- Each of the above needs to be recognized and dealt with in a different way.

8. SUPERVISING

- The successful supervisor must have many skills:

good communication
ability to delegate
responsibility for training
motivation
counselling/advising.

- She (or he) must always be – and be seen to be – loyal to both the team and the company.
- You must be seen to be playing your part as a team member.
- Confront problems as soon as you become aware of them.

9. APPRAISAL

- An appraisal is for the benefit of the employee concerned (and therefore, ultimately, the company). It is not intended to be

an attack on the person involved.
- Its aim is to review progress and discuss the future of the employee.
- An appraisal interview should be an opportunity for two-way discussion.
- There are nine stages to an effective appraisal interview:

1 Prepare properly.
2 Gather information.
3 Complete Part One of an appraisal form; send a copy to the employee in advance.
4 Arrange the interview, allowing ample time.
5 Keep the atmosphere as relaxed as possible.
6 Begin with a discussion of Part One of the form, allowing the employee ample time to ask questions and give feedback.
7 Cover every relevant topic in the course of your discussions.
8 Ask the appraisee how he (or she) feels about the future, keeping your questions open.
9 In the presence of the employee, complete Part Two of the form. Retain one copy and give one to the appraisee.

- Both appraiser and appraisee should spend time analysing the completed form in the time following the interview.

10. DISCIPLINE
- Although disliked by most supervisors, the maintaining of discipline is an essential part of the job.
- A manager/supervisor should be well trained in methods of discipline. If training has been insufficient, request more.
- A full-scale formal disciplinary interview should be viewed as a last resort and should only be conducted when less formal methods have been tried and have failed.
- The manager who is able effectively to discipline an employee when necessary will gain the respect of colleagues at all levels.

- Always keep contemporary notes of all discussions and interviews in case they should be required at a future date.
- Check all facts before reacting. Allow time for tempers to cool.
- During an interview the employee should be given a full and detailed explanation of why she (or he) is there and what goals you would like to reach with her.
- Give the employee plenty of time and attention so that she can put her side of the story. Maintain open body language and ask open questions.
- If the employee obviously believes herself to be in the right, ask yourself:

Are company rules appropriate to the situation?
Were they made clear to the employee?
Is a regular reminder necessary?

- If the problem concerns attitude rather than work, try and find out more about the personal difficulties of the employee.
- If this is something you do not feel equipped to handle, direct the employee to a professionally trained counsellor.
- If any relaxation of the rules is required in this employee's case, explain the situation (without betraying confidences) to other employees so that there is no resentment.
- Write a report immediately after the interview.
- Keep all criticism factual rather than judgemental.
- During the interview:

Keep to the point.
Stay calm.
Maintain a friendly manner.
Make sure the employee does not lose his/her temper.
Be firm.
Keep all questions open-ended.
Don't jump to conclusions.
Avoid personal insults.

Make sure an agreement is reached and conclusions written down and agreed by each of you.

- After the event, provided the employee changes in the agreed way, put the matter behind you.

11. NEGOTIATION

- Negotiation and compromise do not mean that there has to be a winner and a loser.
- Most people do not like the thought of negotiations because:

They assume that compromise means that everyone will be dissatisfied with the outcome.
They fear that either they or the other party will lose their temper.
They fear losing the friendship and/or the respect of the other party.
It is too time-consuming.
They think they would feel humiliated if they were to 'lose'.
They do not want to upset other people.

- Changing the language:

opponents become counterparts
differences become starting-points
arguments become discussions.

- Before negotiations commence, set your own limits (and try and work out what the other person's limits will be).
- Work out any areas where negotiation is not an option.
- Before you begin you should know:

the desired outcome
the acceptable outcome
the boundaries which exist
the time limit
what facts you need at your fingertips

what are the possible 'temptations'.

- Enter negotiations with the right attitude. This is not a battle.
- Be as assertive as possible so that your counterpart realizes you are not 'the enemy'.
- When handling negotiations between yourself and another party:

  Don't rush things.
  Help your counterpart feel good about him- or herself.
  Leave room for negotiation.
  Persuade your counterpart to begin the discussion.
  Don't give in too quickly.
  Say no where essential.
  Keep things friendly.

- When acting as mediator between two (or more) others, arrange a meeting at which all of you can be present.
- Keep this meeting as informal as possible.
- Let the parties know you are aware of a problem and that you will be acting as facilitator rather than making a ruling.
- Allow each to state his point of view to you without interruption. Each should have as much time as needed to explain and to respond.
- Guide the parties through the negotiating process.
- Never allow either party to express anger or to include irrelevant judgemental remarks.
- Encourage your company to provide training in interpersonal and human relations skills.
- Employ a maintenance programme to avoid conflict situations in the future:

  Be observant.
  Improve your own self-esteem.
  Boost the self-esteem of those around you.
  Once a conflict has been resolved, think through the stages and see if there is anything to learn from the process.

Consider arranging regular team forums; the time they take will be justified if they were to prevent conflict in the future.

Bibliography
and Further Information

Jane Allan, *How to Solve Your People Problems* (Kogan Page, 1989)

Dale Carnegie, *How to Win Friends and Influence People* (Simon & Schuster revised edition, 1981)

Elwood N. Chapman, *Improving Relations at Work* (Crisp Publications Inc., 1988)

Helga Drummond, *Managing Difficult Staff* (Kogan Page, 1990)

Rennie Fritchie and Maggie Melling, *The Business of Assertiveness* (BBC Books, 1991)

Carol Kinsey Goman, *Creative Thinking in Business* (Crisp Publications Inc., 1989)

John and Fiona Humphrey, *How to Get More Done* (Kogan Page, 1990)

Herbert S. Kindler, *Managing Disagreement Constructively* (Crisp Publications Inc. 1988)

Ursula Markham, *How to Deal with Difficult People* (Thorsons, 1993)

Allan Pease, *Body Language* (Sheldon Press, 1984)

For details of training courses and staff counselling, contact:
The Hypnothink Foundation
PO Box 66
Gloucester GL2 9YG

Index